In his latest book, Israel Emmanceptionally clear insight into the of Nigerians who, between thei .... and drive to change a nation and impact a continent in a way that will benefit us all. This is a remarkable book, hugely relevant to the Nigerian Diaspora as well as to Nigerian residents. It carries a weight of information that has far wider academic value as well as personal motivating force. I warmly recommend it as a potentially life-transforming and perceptions-expanding read.

- **Dr. Hugh Osgood**, *President, CiC International (UK, Nigeria)*

The Shift of A Lifetime, written by Israel Emmanuel, is a vision to see permanent change in the mindset and attitude of a particular generation of Nigerians – a change that will impact generations to come. Israel's focus is on the power of *significance* and the impact that true self-awareness of one's role in community and society can have on the fulfilment of personal and corporate destiny. This book opens the door to an abundance of possibilities as we take courage to make a difference in our lives and the lives of others. Using Andrew and Duro, readers can easily place themselves in the story and journey with the author into the real life issues that *they* are facing. The great challenge is in determining where the story ends for each of us! *The Shift of A Lifetime* is a book about Nigeria, by a Nigerian for Nigerians in hope of a change.

- **Sola Osinoiki**, *JOSH Publications (UK)*

Israel Emmanuel has aptly reflected the Nigerian Post-independence Generation's huge aspiration for a bright and promising future. He also captured the subsequent socio-economic shift of the 80s that propelled many of them into a new search for a worthwhile means of livelihood, both at home and in Diaspora. *The Shift of A Lifetime* provides the reader with a rich sociological perspective, historical background and contextual analysis of the critical challenges facing, in the author's words, "the Andrew and Duro Generation," and offers a practical and prophetic solution to their dilemmas.

- **Ayo Don-Dawodu BA, MA, Th. D,** *Oasis Chapel (UK)*

This book is a timely prophetic manual and clarion call to a generation called to make a difference in their lifetime. It helps to trace their past history, present reality and future destiny. Israel Emmanuel skilfully defines who we are and highlights what factors have shaped us. He then guides us into how we can fulfil our unique role in history. This book is a must read. I have always said, "If you don't know who you are, other people will call you what you are not." I pray that as you read *The Shift of A Lifetime*, you will discover your real place in destiny.

- **Dr. Sola Fola-Alade**, *Trinity Chapel (UK), Publisher of Leadership & Lifestyle magazine*

I thought Bob Buford had said the last word on the concept of Halftime. How wrong can one get! If you are at that crossroad in your life where you are asking the question, 'What next?,' this is a book you *must* read. In simple but compelling language, Israel has vividly captured the dilemma of a generation in search of definition. From a well-contextualized dimension, he has provided a refreshing and instructive bent to the concept of Halftime and the journey towards Significance. Taking this beyond the individual and stretching it to cover the need for a national reawakening and collective transformation through individual and collective soul-searching coupled with definitive action, the author helps us to navigate and bridge the chasm between success and significance. In doing that, he also underscores one vital fact that many in Generation D discover sometimes too late; every good and perfect gift is from *above*, not from *abroad*! If I had my way, I would make this compulsory reading for every Nigerian from the age of 18!

- **Tope Popoola**, *Pastor, Human Capital Development Consultant and Author of the Bestseller "Living Intentionally" (Nigeria)*

The Shift of A Lifetime by Israel Emmanuel, is a classic; the product of well-researched and well-articulated facts addressed primarily to different generations of Nigerians. It has certainly come at this hour to help us shake off the dust of a regressive mindset so that we may all fit perfectly into what God has ordained for our lives and our nation.

Whatever generation we belong, the one ultimate truth that should stand above the rest in our hearts is that a life without purpose and significance is vanity. Israel chronicles this when he said, "The conclusion of someone who only labours for 'success' is likely to be, 'Vanity of vanities; all is vanity'". In view of this understanding, he challenges us to subscribe to *Significance* instead of *Success*—the only way to fulfil the greatest reason for our existence, which is influence.

I believe this special work will help the present generation to understand what life is about and how to find true meaning to it. I believe too that the previous generation can learn from the truths enumerated here and salvage whatever is left of their time on the Earth. *The Shift of A Lifetime* tells me that there is still hope for the hopeless. The author's appeal for a change of paradigm is both important and instructive—and must be embraced if we truly desire to realise our individual and national potential.

- **Bishop Abraham Olaleye** *Abraham's Evangelistic Ministry (Nigeria)*

The Shift of A Lifetime is a prophetic word to a nation at crossroads. With a sense of disillusionment about the future of our nation, the young generation wonders if their dreams of a great Nigeria will not be a mirage at the end of their lives. But this book is a God-sent message of hope, sharp reflection on the past and present, clear road map for the future to give the Nigerian reader and our dear country courage in despair and strength to birth a new Nigeria.

Rev. Victor Adeyemi, *Global Harvest Church (Nigeria)*

This book is the work of a social philosopher. I am persuaded that it will be a much-quoted material by many seeking to stream a light on the malaise eating through Sub-Saharan Africa as a canker. Israel's new book so accurately pinpoints the issues facing Nigerians, and also gives appropriate solutions. I advise anyone seeking to buy a present for any "Generation D" to please buy this book.

- Success Oso, *Living Realities Ministries (UK)*

Personally, I regard Israel Emmanuel highly as one of the gifted Christian writers of our time. His books are not mere knowledge, but true revelations.

- Pastor Sunday Adelaja, *Embassy of God (Ukraine)*

THE SHIFT
OF A LIFETIME

MOVING A GENERATION FROM SURVIVAL TO SIGNIFICANCE

ISRAEL EMMANUEL

Raising the voice of Wisdom!

The Shift of A Lifetime
Copyright © 2010 by Israel Adetokunbo Emmanuel

Published by
Sophos Books
15 North Downs Road
Croydon
CR0 0LE
United Kingdom

In Nigeria:
150 Adebowale House
Onipan Bus Stop, Ikorodu Road
Lagos
Tel: 0703 6203291

Sophos Books is an imprint of GPS

Distributed by
Books With A Mission
http://www.bookswithamission.org

All rights reserved. No part of this publication may be reproduced, stored in a retrieval system, or transmitted in any form or by any means, mechanical, electronic photocopying or otherwise without prior written consent of the copyright owner.

ISBN 13: 978-1-905669-20-2

Cover design by Michael Masade Jr.

Printed in the United Kingdom

CONTENTS

Dedication **9**
Acknowledgements **11**
Author's Preface **13**
Foreword **15**
Introduction **19**

SECTION I: History
1. The Profile of Survival **29**
2. In Pursuit of Success **37**
3. Generation D **47**

SECTION II: Reality
4. It is Halftime! **63**
5. Survival, Success or Significance? **81**
6. The Significance Shift **99**

SECTION III: Destiny
7. Life Begins After Halftime! **113**
8. Can A Nation Shift? **133**
9. The Coming Transformation **153**

Conclusion **171**
Appendix **175**
End Notes **179**
Index **185**

*To the future of Nigeria
and Nigerians everywhere*

ACKNOWLEDGEMENTS

A work like this does not just happen. Life prepares you for it. The first half of my life did exactly that to me — I was just not aware of the depth of preparation that was occurring. Inevitably, some special people take part in the preparation process. For me, that's everyone I have known to date — in and outside Nigeria. My gratitude goes to you all for the role you have played in my life.

For the sake of specificity, I am grateful to my parents, Deacon Kunle Odulaja (late) and Pastor (Mrs.) Esther Olulaja, for their care during the preparatory years. To my mum-in-law, Cornelia Okuleye, for accomplishing the same in the life of my wife. Dr. Hugh Osgood added much value to this work, just as he has to my life over the years. Dr. Sunday Adelaja has taught me a great deal about true significance. Thanks to Pastor Success and Olivia Oso for being a rock solid help during my transition months. The same goes to Pastor David and Sola Olorunniwo. And "Thank you" to everyone who gave helpful feedback after reading initial drafts of this book. Special thanks to Rev. Sam Adeyemi for his insightful foreword. Also to Toyin Oladele, for proof-reading the final draft.

I am eternally grateful to the wife of my youth, Linda, who is still "shifting" alongside me on this journey towards significance. Moreover, she blessed me with our third child, David, four days before my fortieth birthday—the best birthday present ever. Life can truly begin at forty!

To Destiny, Daniel and David, thank you for the joy and meaning you bring to each day, and for giving Daddy the space to write and write some more.

Finally, I could not have written a single line without the inspiration of my Creator and Lord. This work is yours. Now use it for your glory.

AUTHOR'S PREFACE

*I*t was July, 2009 and I was riding on the Bus 64, heading for East Croydon, South East London. Without any premonition, I began to have a brain wave. Thankfully, I had a notebook in which I quickly scribbled my thoughts. The more I ruminated on the concept I jotted down, the more I realised God was giving me a message for my generation and my nation. *The Shift of A Lifetime* is the fruit of that day's experience.

I started writing beginning of 2010 after a few months of churning the message over. Whenever I discussed it with friends, they agreed this was an urgent and relevant subject. The happenings in

Nigeria around the time I started writing also confirmed this sentiment.[1] I am not a sociologist, historian, academician or politician. I am simply a messenger with a pen. This timely message is now being delivered to you. It could be one of the most important messages you will receive in a lifetime.

I enjoyed writing this book and have experienced a fresh beginning in my writing and publishing vocation. I trust you will not only enjoy reading *The Shift of A Lifetime*, but also have your own experience of a new beginning in life.

Israel Emmanuel
1 March, 2010

FOREWORD

Fantastic! That is the word that flashed in my mind severally as I raced through the pages of *The Shift of a Lifetime*. It is, without doubt, a classic.

Abraham Maslow placed human needs on five levels. First, the need for food, drink and sleep. Second, the need for security, essentially shelter. On the third level, humans have need for love and belonging. On the fourth level is the need for self-esteem, fostered by the acquisition of skill. And the highest is the need for *significance*, fulfilled by adding value to others. The needs on the first two levels are material. They are survival needs. The instinct for survival is the strongest in us humans. When those needs are not met, we tend to focus all our spiritual, mental and physical resources on acquiring material provision. In fact, meeting those needs can become the greatest objectives in our lives.

The deep deprivation caused by the regression in Nigeria's socio-economic situation especially in the last two decades has put most of her citizens, both at home and in Diaspora, in survival mode. The impact has been devastating on the family, governance, the economy and even our spiritual lives. Success has been defined for us only in terms of material acquisition. Political leaders, with the fight for survival etched deeply in their sub-conscious, have used leadership positions to secure their future and that of their children, using public funds to enrich themselves while further impoverishing the people they are meant to empower. The message of prosperity, which would have transformed the country, if like Christians in the Bible we used our resources to solve problems for the community, only served to fuel self-centeredness and greed, beginning with spiritual leaders. Our values have been eroded. It is now obvious to most, that there is a disconnect somewhere.

How do you meet your need for food, drink and shelter? Hear what Jesus said; *"Therefore I say to you, do not worry about your life, what you will eat or what you will drink; or about your body, what you will put on. Is not life more than food and the body more than clothing? ... But seek first the kingdom of God and His righteousness, and all these things shall be added to you."* (Matthew 6:25,33). My understanding is that you go first for the highest level, *Significance*, and your material needs will be met. And your need for a feeling of significance is met when you solve problems for people. If we want to succeed God's way, we must align our values to those of Jesus. We must focus on feeding others, creating housing, loving people and ensuring there is justice.

The developed nations to which Nigerians run or seek to run have collectively ensured that the needs for food and shelter are met for their citizens with minimum effort. Their citizens have then been able to focus their energies on intangibles like value for life, value for knowledge, value for time, innovation, excellence, courtesy, justice and service to others. Looking from that perspective, rather than run away from Nigeria's problems, we should see them as our best opportunity to live life at the highest level. We must not throw away powerful values like honesty, love, justice, contentment and service only to make money. Without those values, we don't have value. No amount of huge contracts will ever get our country developed.

I resolved recently that I would embark on a crusade for the cultivation and restoration of biblical values, both by the sermons I preach and by my way of life. And just then; bang! Israel Emmanuel requested for me to write the foreword to *The Shift of a Lifetime*. And I said 'fantastic' over and over as I read all the way through. It is well-researched. It is life-changing. It will give every Nigerian a paradigm shift. Well then, this book *is* the crusade!

If there is a book you need to read at least twice in a year for the next five years, this is it. And by the way, though it is intended for Nigerians in mid-life right now, every Nigerian needs to read it. Then he or she must rise to the occasion. We must confront the things in our culture, our environment and our policies that hold us back, and we must create a new Nigeria. We must be willing to sacrifice. We must do so with the hope that we can look back in thirty or forty years with fulfilment. Real success is not measured by how much we acquire but by how much we give. God will help us.

Sam Adeyemi
Success Power International

INTRODUCTION

Our world continues to change at an exponential rate. Arguably, societal transformations in the first ten years of the 21st Century transcend those of any decade in the 20th. In most cases, these changes do not just happen. A combination of events and personalities constitute the seeds for dramatic shifts that seem to "suddenly" come upon the world. Those who through the study of what has been and what is transpiring at the moment can safely predict what might be (and recommend what ought to be done).

The religious amongst men, who constitute a sizeable part of humanity, attribute global phenomena to the aged pronouncements of Deity. They assert that God's Word is absolute and infallible; it will always find fulfilment in the course of time. By implication, the seeds of tomorrow's changes are hidden in the context of history (past events) or prophecy (God's pronouncements), or both. It is wise, then, to devote time to studying what yesterday has to teach us about tomorrow, either from historic or prophetic viewpoints.

The Western World, it seems, pays better attention to societal trends than the developing world. They are committed to documenting and archiving events, no matter how trivial, and spend considerable amounts of time and resources scrutinising them. They value the contribution of social commentators and their analysis of society, whether observational or scientific. Governments factor their findings into their policy development programmes. Entrepreneurs use them to determine profitable ventures. Religious leaders us them to guide their congregations. The common man ignores them to his own peril. Those who see change before it arrives have the opportunity to take full advantage of it and benefit immensely, while the rest of society merely react.

GENERATIONAL STUDIES

Let us take generational studies as an example, the study of how particular groups in a given society have developed in relation to the rest of society. A point in question is the popularised generational groupings that define the behavioural patterns of certain aspects of American sub-cultures. These include the *Baby Boomer Generation* (1945 – 1960), which refers to the group born after World War II; *Generation X* (early 1960s – late 1970s); *Generation Y* or *Generation Next* (1980 – mid 1990s); *Generation Z* (mid 1990s – late 2000s).[1] These groupings have characteristics and worldviews that are peculiar to them. As mentioned earlier, the West's interest and understanding of these distinctions have proved helpful in determining trends, improving cross-generational interaction, sustaining national development and making adequate preparation for the future. In addition, since the happenings in America, whether good or bad, affect the entire world in one way or the other, the wider global community is interested in these studies as well.

The seeds of tomorrow's changes are hidden in the context of history (past events) or prophecy (God's pronouncements), or both.

Instinctively, every culture has an understanding of its own generational groupings, and indigenous social commentators broadcast the obvious to its masses for the common good. The extent to which any nation's sub-cultures affect the world is the extent to which the rest of the world would show an interest in studying or referring to them. For instance, China's Generation Y, those born between 1980 and 1989 in urban areas of Mainland China fit into this category. The mere size of China and her growing economic strength makes the study of this and other Chinese groups a necessity. It provides vital clues to some of the corporate shifts that are taking place, and are likely to occur between the West and the East.

NIGERIA: A FRESH FOCUS

My focus in this book is on a particular group of people. They are not from New England, Europe or Asia. They are not based in Australia, the Americas or the Middle East. They are a people who originate from sub-Saharan Africa and reside in virtually every part of the world. I am referring to the Nigerian people, citizens of the most populous Black Country in the world.[2] As we will soon see, the fate of the Nigerian people should interest the world because it has potential worldwide consequences.

Unfortunately, sociological studies of Nigeria's sub-cultures are not in wide circulation. The ones that exist are in the form of special papers or academic researches; they have not made their way into the wider print media. Writings about the Civil War (1967 – 1970), for instance, abound, but studies about its effect on the Nigerian people, particularly the generation that witnessed or participated in it, are not a global phenomena. Even though this lack of processed knowledge does not reduce the peculiarity of this period or its distinctive impact on the Nigerian mind at the time and now, its scarce existence robs future generations of vital information.

In my opinion, the way Nigerians influence the world is not given enough attention. This is not so much the fault of the global community, but that of the very nation from which they hail. The world would only place on us the value that we place on ourselves. If we do not esteem ourselves and believe in our own importance, others will place any label on us as they deem fit. Nonetheless, I maintain that the factors that influence the mind of a Nigerian and inform his choices are worth analysing because of their potential impact on the Globe.

The Shift of A Lifetime seeks to create a broad awareness of this subject in the popular media. It will focus on a particular group of Nigerians, those born between 1960 (or just before then) and 1970 (or just after then). What are their characteristics and peculiarities? What are the unique experiences that have shaped their thinking? What are the dilemmas that they face and how will their choices affect their global counterparts? Exploring their *brief history* and *unfulfilled prophecies* would give us some insight into their *emerging destiny*.

The world would only place on us the value that we place on ourselves. If we do not esteem ourselves and believe in our own importance, others will place any label on us as they deem fit.

Moreover, if there is any truth in the notion that their choices in the coming years can affect the entire world (or sizeable sections of it), then these observations are worth exploring. I belong to this generation and know so well the challenges before us. We are no longer growing adults, but are now at an age that calls for reflection and responsibility. My generation has a lot of thinking to do and more importantly, major decisions to make.

BETWEEN SURVIVAL AND SIGNIFICANCE

Put simply, we are at the crossroads of *Survival, Success* and *Significance*. This is not a minor junction but a major split in direction that requires clear convictions about one's preferred destination. Because these diverging routes do not lead to the same place – the goal called *Satisfaction and Fulfilment* – we cannot take this time lightly. There is no better time to pause and consider destiny than mid-life.

The Shift of A Lifetime, I hope, will help the thought process and provide a context for the inevitable decisions we have to make at this time. It will also show the personal, national and global ramifications of the many issues we face. In the same way that the sociological impact of the American *Baby Boomer* has affected the world, especially the global financial institutions, my generation has not only impacted the nations of the world, it is poised to cause a major shift in the coming times. This assertion underscores the urgency of this assignment.

The Shift of A Lifetime is in three sections. The first section (*History*) will give a brief overview of the plight of the generation in question. The second section (*Reality*) will guide the reader in analysing his current state and discovering his unrealised potential. The third section (*Destiny*) will point to the future and encourage a shift in the right direction.

I have not written to provide *comprehensive answers* to every query but to ask *enough questions* that will stir up a quest for individual and national significance. It is my hope nonetheless, that you will find this book *informative, interactive* and ultimately *inspiring*. The issues it addresses concerns us all—male, female, young and old.

Well, let's get started!

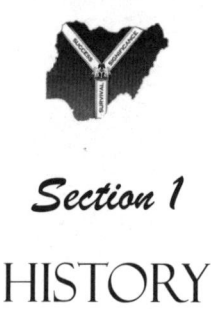

Section 1

HISTORY

Chapter 1

THE PORTRAIT OF SURVIVAL

I want you to meet Andrew and his fellow Nigerian, Duro. They were born only a few years apart, Andrew in 1966 and Duro four years afterwards. These birth years put them in the same generational grouping that we want to explore in this book (people born between 1960 and 1970, plus or minus two years at each end).

Andrew and Duro's parents are of the generation that favoured self-rule and pressured the colonial rulers toward national independence. This was a growing Continent-wide aspiration at the time that gathered momentum after the 2nd World War.

The expectations of Nigerians were eventually realised on October 1, 1960, by which time the Post-Independence Generation, born roughly between 1935 and 1950, were ready to start forming new family units. Although not our primary focus, understanding the circumstances that shaped this older generation may help us better understand their children, the Andrew and Duro Generation.[1]

THE POST-INDEPENDENCE GENERATION

The Post-Independence Generation, were just children when the 2nd World War finally ended in the summer of 1945. Although the Nigerian territory was not a direct conflict zone and Nigerians were largely civilian spectators, the British colonial masters of the time were heavily involved around the world.

The Pre-Independence Generation, parents of the Post-Independence Generation, kept abreast of the global conflict through their radio sets, as televisions were not in wide circulation at time. This voice-only device kept the Nigerian masses informed of global events and fuelled the support they gave to the independence advocates. Now a Federal Republic, both young and old looked forward to the future under the leadership of Govenor-General Nnamde Azikiwe.

Soon after independence, a wide door opened for the Post-Independence Generation to travel *en masse* to Britain, mainly for study purposes. It was expedient that a crop of young Nigerians acquired the best education in order to fill the gaps that the white man would leave after independence. Bright minds were also required for the future development of Nigeria. Scholarships to study abroad were widely available. Well-to-do Pre-Independence parents were also proud to send their children overseas. As a member of the British Commonwealth, Nigerians did not require a visa to travel to the UK during this time.

EMERGING DICHOTOMY

Most of these young students, upon arriving in the UK, began to form new family units with fellow students who also came to study or lovers who came to join them abroad. Before long, the first set of children came. Now, since these children were born on British-soil, they automatically had British Citizenship, making them both Nigerian and British at the same time. Back home, the offspring of those who did not travel abroad remained single-nationality children—a disparity that would not prove important for another decade.

Meanwhile, the Post-Independence Generation studying abroad endeavoured to follow the news of what was happening at home. They followed the good and the bad of Nigeria's post-independence through the media and expensive long-distance telephone calls. Tribal tensions, coup d'états and the Civil War (1967 – 1970) dominated the first decade of freedom. The oil boom of the seventies followed this traumatic time, and Nigeria began to flourish tremendously. The Post-Independence Generation that stayed at home were now enjoying the best of times, while those who travelled, who were now completing their studies and seeking work experience, longed to partake of the party. They had endured the cold of Britain, held multiple odd jobs to earn a living and managed to cope with racial discrimination that was rife in British society at the time. They were survivors in a foreign land who longed for a freedom of their own!

Having been away from their homeland for a long time, they had become homesick. They missed everything about Nigeria. There were ageing parents to see (and some to bury); there were siblings and old friends to reunite with; they longed for "proper" food with pepper soup; they looked forward to better job prospects and business opportunities that would provide income for their young families. Besides, they were Nigerian passport holders and had a duty to develop their country with the knowledge they now possessed. All these circumstances combined to create the common mindset of the Post-Independence Generation that lived abroad. Envisioning a good life back home, they had every reason to uproot their young families in pursuit of it.

Back home, the offspring of those who did not travel abroad remained single-nationality children—a disparity that would not prove important for another decade.

Reintegrating into Nigeria had its challenges but it was a welcome transition. Seemingly, there was enough national wealth to facilitate the shift. As anticipated, the returning workforce found jobs and started businesses. They also went on to round up their childbearing goals. Six was an average family size in those days, just counting the children, and they had come back with half the number. This created an interesting dichotomy in Post-Independence Nigeria. A section of society had travelled and studied abroad, while the other had not; and in almost all the families of the Returning Generation, half the children were British-born, while half was not. Again, this sociological divide would be of great significance in the coming years.

BEGINNINGS OF SOCIETAL DILAPIDATION

In the meantime, the Niger-Delta oil was feeding the nation, funding grand events like FESTAC '77,[2] and fuelling the greed of the political elite. The growing clamour for an end to military rule led to the elections of 1979 and the beginning of the second Republic, with Alhaji Shehu Shagari sworn in as President. The majority of the Andrew and Duro Generation were too young to vote during this election. The factors that were shaping society around them were outside their control. Even their parents could only look on as the country they loved took an economic and political nosedive. In the space of four years, Nigeria went from the glories of national prosperity to the ashes of national poverty, a situation that led to yet another military intervention.

The older Pre-Independence ruling elite and Post-Independence working class were preoccupied with the twists and turns of national life. Largely, they neglected the growing Andrew and Duro Generation, now in their early teens and early twenties. This emerging cohort did not inherit any national vision from the older generation neither was there much opportunity for them to play any significant role in national development. As stated earlier, they were largely uninvolved in the voting process during the 1979 elections, and with the military now in power, the prospect of an imminent return to democracy was bleak. Happenings around them, both nationally and internationally, were shaping their perceptions and convictions. Naturally, they gravitated towards the music of Fela Kuti, the outspokenness of Gani Fawehinmi and the writings of Dele Giwa and Wole Soyinka, all who were political activists.

In the space of four years, Nigeria went from the glories of national prosperity to the ashes of national poverty.

Now at the age of reason, rebellion and increased political awareness, students debated on campuses, staged protests and clashed with mobile police. Most of this generation were against IMF[3] loans and did not see the sense in the Government's Structural Adjustment Programmes. What could they do? What future did Nigeria hold for them? The Government punished them almost every year for their critical stance by closing their Universities for months at a time (and when it was not the Government, it was their lecturers who were protesting against low incomes and poor working conditions). The Utopia their parents dreamt of was fading. The Naira-

Pound-Dollar foreign exchange rates were soaring. Nigeria was struggling to survive.

It was during this time in the early 80s that the future of Andrew and Duro took diverging paths. The difference in their countries of birth was the main distinction that determined their fate. Andrew, owing to his dual nationality status, would nurse the idea of escaping the sinking ship called Nigeria and returning to his second country. Duro, the single nationality youngster, would stay behind, but not for too long.

Chapter 2

IN PURSUIT
OF SUCCESS

"Men! I'm checking out. No good roads, no light, no water. Men! You can't even get a common bottle of soft drink..."

The above is an excerpt from the widely televised media campaign by the Nigerian Government to discourage Andrew and others of his generation from deserting Nigeria. The aim of the campaign, which was to preserve the next generation of Nigeria's educated workforce, was commendable, but it was grossly ineffective in convincing this Fleeing Generation to prioritise the development of their country. If those who wanted them to stay did not portray such a priority, why should they? Stories that permeated the grassroots focused on how the military rulers were looting the National Treasury and stashing up cash for themselves in foreign banks. They were equally as bad as the civilians they took over from, if not worse. What was the logic of staying to invest into the future of Nigeria when those who were at the helm of power had already stolen huge chunks of it? The chances of a University graduate landing a good job after his National Youth Service were dwindling. The increasingly corrupt system did not reward you based on merit, but on association and behind-the-door negotiations. All these contributed to a major exodus from Nigeria, beginning with Andrew and those who suddenly realised they had privileges in a more civilised country.

ANDREW "CHECKS OUT"!

All that Andrew needed to do to travel to the United Kingdom was present his Birth Certificate as proof that he was born in Britain. With this important document, the British Consulate gave Andrew the right to abide indefinitely in the United Kingdom. It was that simple. Returning to Britain, Andrew discovered that this 'right' also came with the promise of a place to live and a weekly allowance, all paid for by the British Government. When news of this 'better life' filtered through to the other 'Andrews' in

Nigeria, it was only a matter of time before they all began to relocate abroad. This was the beginning of a massive generational shift that the Nigerian Government could not prevent.

The Andrew and Duro Generation now considered living abroad the key to their survival. It could also be the path that led to "success". In terms of economic empowerment, it made perfect sense (prevailing circumstances had conditioned them to reason in monetary terms). The Naira was falling in value and the Pound was strong. Any income overseas was worth much more in Nigeria, not to mention the perfect living conditions of constant power and water supply. So, while Nigeria deteriorated, the Andrew and Duro Generation occupied itself with how to "check out" of the country.

The spouses-to-be of the Fleeing Generation, many of whom were Nigerian-born, had a relatively easy passage. Their lovers came back home to marry them and subsequently apply for their visas to remain indefinitely with them abroad. Finding a British Citizen to marry soon became a popular way of gaining British status. Arranged marriages with the prospect of securing the right to stay in the UK were now on the rise, some for large sums of money. In short, these turn of events birthed another 'industry' among the Andrew and Duro Generation – the Visa Application industry! The cry of most people was, 'I am a Nigerian, get me out of here!' Anywhere would do but the Nigerian territory.

For every legitimate way of travelling abroad, which many people successfully explored, enterprising Nigerians created numerous unlawful alternatives. Bogus schools sprung up in the UK through which people could apply for student visas. A highly effective virtual immigration bureau, popularly known as *Oluwole*, helped many with travel documents. Some travelled out of the country as house helps, while others risked their lives through the Sahara desert of North Africa and the waters of the Mediterranean Sea.

While Nigeria deteriorated, the Andrew and Duro Generation occupied itself with how to "check out" of the country.

Countries like the UK and USA, needing the economic contribution of foreigners, created schemes to assimilate the highly skilled, and many bright and well-educated Nigerians took full advantage of the opportunity. In addition, thousands of Nigerians began to apply for the yearly American visa lottery with many lucky enough to make their escape through this avenue. The *means* of travelling abroad was not as important as the *end* of getting there. Before the overseas countries could clamp down on the influx of immigrants, hundreds of thousands of Nigerians were already living amongst them. The rate at which they could deport those who had come in illegally was much less than the rate at which others were coming in. In less than two decades, more than a million Nigerians had come to live in the USA and UK alone, not counting huge Diaspora communities in other Western, Asian and even other African countries.

This pursuit of success and a better life, even at the expense of development in the home country, is understandable. The Andrew and Duro Generation had to take their destinies in their own hands and chart a pathway for themselves. The older generation were not doing it for them. Their flight was a basic, self-preserving characteristic of humankind. What else could they do? How would they cater for the new families they were going to start forming when unemployment was rising and the nation was unstable? They had to find a way and it was not on Nigerian soil.

SURVIVAL IN A FOREIGN LAND

Arriving in their destinations, the energetic Andrew and Duro Generation put their industrious minds to use straightaway. Success, however perceived, does not come without a price, especially in developed societies. Generally, the average Nigerian is ready to pay the price, whatever it entails. For many just arriving, it meant doing odd jobs at odd hours, sometimes two or three in a day. This was necessary to pay for rent and school fees.

In the UK, those who already had the Right of Abode had somewhat of a head-start over their fellow Nigerians. Their status meant they were entitled to Social Security benefits in terms of weekly Giro cheques, paid considerably less in school fees and soon had a council flat in which to live. They also received monthly benefits from the Government for every child that was born. Unfortunately, a few found a variety of ways to exploit this generous welfare system by using multiple identities to receive multiple benefits, justifying their deception by claiming it was payback time for Colonial Britain. While this seemed to quicken the attainment of success in terms of money in the bank, it also tainted the general perception of Nigerians in the minds of others.

Not every Nigerian, of course, is dubious. The truth is most are enterprising and hardworking. Many who had completed their first degrees at home painfully endured the adaptation process required for them to practice their profession abroad. These now occupy reputable positions in their different fields, especially in the USA, where weekly social benefits are not the norm.

Apart from securing professional positions, the Andrew and Duro Generation in Diaspora continued to explore every opportunity for acquiring wealth. They entered the Civil Service and Local Councils, went *en masse* into IT and Project Management, and got involved in Network Marketing and property businesses. The list goes on. For those who could afford it, the pursuit of success also meant buying a property in their adopted country and building one back home. Many began to purchase land in Nigeria's big cities, a feat the peers they left at home could not readily accomplish. Occasional visits to Nigeria, especially during holidays and family events, were a time to show off the "success" of living abroad – made possible by the falling Naira and the more powerful foreign currency. This only raised the level of desperation for travelling abroad in the mind of those living in Nigeria.

SURVIVAL AT HOME

The pursuit of success by the Andrew and Duro Generation living in Nigeria was a different reality. Faced with a collapsing educational system, dwindling opportunities and a failing Government, they had to survive at any cost. Many young women in college and University traded their bodies to make ends meet. Young men put their resourceful abilities to task, and developed what had become a global phenomenon – the 419 epidemic.[1] (Advance-fee frauds are not associated with Nigerians alone; they have been practised in different societies around the world and called different names.[2] Nonetheless, the widespread awareness and impact of '419 frauds' is just an example of how the peculiarities of a generation of Nigerians have global ramifications). Bribery and corruption were infecting the whole of Nigerian-based society and it was easier to flow with the trend than try to beat it. People became used to the unreliability of NEPA,[3] the ineffectiveness of the civil service, the selfishness of national leaders, the constant closure of tertiary institutions and the deterioration of society's infrastructure. Nigeria became a jungle where only the fittest could survive.

The widespread awareness and impact of '419 frauds' is just an example of how the peculiarities of a generation of Nigerians have global ramifications.

Fela's *Shuffering and Shmiling*, written in 1978, provides a relevant depiction of everyday society at this time:

> Everyday my people dey inside bus
>
> Forty-nine sitting, ninety-nine standing
>
> Them go pack themselves in like sardine
>
> Them dey faint, them dey wake like cock
>
> Them go reach house, water no dey
>
> Them go reach bed, power no dey
>
> Them go reach road, go-slow go come
>
> Them go reach road, police go slap
>
> Them go reach road, army go whip
>
> Them go look pocket, money no dey
>
> Them go reach work, query ready
>
> Everyday na the same thing
>
> Everyday na the same thing

In the following chapter, we will explore a bit more closely some of the unique experiences that have shaped the perspectives of the Andrew and Duro Generation, and are bound to influence their future, the future of Nigeria and that of the world.

Chapter 3

GENERATION D

So far, we have conducted a brief overview of the prevailing circumstances that led to the shaping of the Andrew and Duro Generation. In this chapter, we will look a bit more closely at the plight of this generation, especially those who were lucky enough to travel out of Nigeria, and propose, as the chapter title suggests, a description that may well suit its characteristics. I am calling my generation the D Generation (or Generation D) because of the many D-words that describe our sojourn to date.

DISPERSED GENERATION

We have already seen one of the obvious features of this generation – the way they are *Dispersed* to the four corners of the Earth. This is a generation in *Diaspora*. Discounting the forced exodus of Africans, Nigerians included, during the era of slavery, the Andrew and Duro Generation is the second wave of Nigerians to travel in droves out of Nigeria; the first being the expeditions of the 1960s. Unlike the first wave, who left Nigeria mainly to study, this second wave of Nigerians "checked out" of Nigeria primarily because of the dilapidation of Nigerian society. Nigerians in Diaspora (NID), as they are widely called, now total in excess of three million and reside in almost every country in the world.[1]

There are stark differences between the first and second wave of NIDs. The Post-Independence Nigerian in Diaspora came to study and had the mind of returning to their oil-rich country. Today's NID left Nigeria in frustration with no definite return date in mind. The unstoppable decline in Nigeria's political and economic infrastructure during the Babangida and Abacha regimes[2] further obliterated the thought of returning. NIDs are now well-settled in their adopted countries and are raising the next generation of dual-citizen Nigerians, many of whom have not yet visited Nigeria once.

DESPERATE GENERATION

The Andrew and Duro Generation is a *Desperate* generation. Survival and the pursuit of success are not casual games that spare the lives of their players. Those who fall by the wayside end up downtrodden by their fellow compatriots. Desperate for survival, the NID settled for any kind of work on offer, ranging from cleaning toilets to driving taxis. Professionals went through all sorts of stress adapting their professional status to Western standards. Those who were stuck at home sought every means for making ends meet. Many gravitated towards the big cities in search of jobs. Many took to cyber cafes where they perfected the Nigerian brand of "Advance fee" methodologies. Drug trafficking also escalated as an easy way to escape the rat race.

DEPRIVED GENERATION

Looking back, the Andrew and Duro Generation feels *Deprived*. Their parents did not allow them to follow their hearts' passion. Coming from the old school of read-your-books-and-earn-a-good-living, Post-Independent Nigerians discouraged their children from pursuing their fields of interest. They wanted their children to follow *their* example and become doctors, lawyers, engineers, accountants and teachers, thus hindering those who had the talent and interest in sports, acting, singing and dancing. If only they could foresee the day when footballers would earn hefty weekly salaries and *Nollywood* entertainers would become famous the world over. Nowadays, parents encourage their children to play football alongside their studies – just in case!

DISAPPOINTED GENERATION

Obviously, the Andrew and Duro Generation is grossly *Disappointed* with the performance of the nation's politicians. After nearly fifty years of independence from British rule, Nigeria's political elite have not cared to deliver on their many promises of national development and prosperity for all. Instead, they have systematically decimated the nation and siphoned her abundant resources for themselves, leaving the masses in abject poverty. Multi-layered bureaucracy has weaved corruption into the fabric of day-to-day society. Basic social amenities, especially the availability of power, are nowhere comparable with what entails in the developed world. If there is a single reason why the Andrew and Duro Generation living abroad would shun returning back home, and why those living in Nigeria, given the opportunity, would choose to "check out", this is the one. Hardly any of the little things that make life relatively bearable work in Nigeria. The disappointment is not just in the fact that they do not work, but also in the knowledge that we have the potential to make them work. In spite of all her intellectuals and natural blessedness, Nigeria, the beloved country, continues to underperform.

After nearly fifty years of independence from British rule, Nigeria's political elite have not cared to deliver on their many promises of national development and prosperity for all.

DETACHED GENERATION

Although the Andrew and Duro Generation abroad remains emotionally attached to its country, not least because of the relatives and friends it has left behind, it is now increasingly *Detached* from happenings in the nation. This is due to the length of time it has spent away from home. Add to this the ever-increasing gap in its comparison between life in Diaspora and the two-weeks-in-three-years that it manages to spend at home. This detachment is more pronounced among its children who know they are Nigerian by descent but identify more with being British or American (or whatever happens to be the nationality of their birth). Their accent speaks volumes in their defence. Unlike the Post-Independence Nigerian who returned to Nigeria in the 70s, the Andrew and Duro Generation cannot just uproot their families and return home because their children are much older than when they returned with their parents. It is easier to relocate a child into a different culture when he or she is six than when he or she is twelve or eighteen.

This detachment leaves a feeling of helplessness and frustration in members of the Andrew and Duro Generation. Whilst they loathe the ugliness of affairs in the nation, they cannot actively participate in correcting its bad points (other than express their opinions through writing and in different forums) or directly partake of the good developments sprouting in different quarters.

DESTITUTE GENERATION

One of the unique features of the overseas-based Andrew and Duro Generation, unlike its counterparts at home, is that this is a generation living in *Debt*; a *Destitute* generation indeed. When they left their countries for the more developed nations, no one had prepared them for the culture of debt that is the bedrock of Western society. From their 1980s experience of Nigeria, they knew a bit about *national* debt, but not *personal* debt. In a race to acquire the comforts of life, they bit the bait of easy financing and piled up debt to many creditors. They bought freely yesterday and are now paying heavily today. Although they hardly communicate this to their folks at home, the Andrew and Duro Generation has to work round the clock not because they *love to*, but because they *have to*. They have to pay for all the things bought on credit. Earning a reasonable salary, even as a highly-skilled professional, does not make much difference because the higher the income, the more the tendency to pile up the credit, thus reducing disposable income considerably. Building a house in Nigeria and owning one in the West are two worlds apart. The former is already paid for whilst the other is still being paid for with sweat. If only the full story were told, that life in the West is not a bed of roses.

A GENERATION BURDENED WITH DEPENDANTS

One of the monthly 'bills' that the Andrew and Duro Generation labours to pay is the support of their *Dependants* back home. A "dependant" here does not refer to their children alone, but also siblings, parents and other extended family members. The massive money transfer business is the lifesaver of many relatives of the Andrew and Duro Generation. Even the vegetable trader in the market square knows the going foreign exchange rate! Both the givers and the receivers seem to consider this monthly support system as the cost of being apart for so long. It feeds the emotional attachment that NIDs feel towards Nigeria and the sense of belonging as a Nigerian. An after-feeling, however, is a sense of indeterminate enslavement.

DUPED GENERATION

It is not uncommon for some relatives of the Andrew and Duro Generation to *Dupe* their overseas breadwinners. All they need to do is cook up a story (usually sickness in the family), send a text and await some Western Union details. There are many instances where relatives collect large sums of money for capital projects on the sender's behalf – projects that never materialise. This familiar *Deception* has created enemies amongst family members and popularised the notion that "You cannot trust anyone in Nigeria, not even your flesh and blood."

If only the full story were told, that life in the West is not a bed of roses.

DISILLUSIONED GENERATION

Another feature of the Andrew and Duro Generation, both at home and abroad, is the feeling of *Disillusionment* with religion. Coinciding with the exodus of the 1980s was the rise of popular Christianity that promised success and prosperity to believers. All over the nation, the "Prosperity Gospel", perhaps due to the widespread hardship that many were enduring, was appealing to more people compared with traditional, conservative doctrines, and churches began to imbibe this teaching to different degrees. Before long, church programmes shifted their focus from an eternal to a material emphasis, guaranteeing attendees a relief from hardship and miraculous breakthroughs in their finances – a welcome message for those who were struggling to *survive* and striving to *succeed*. Generally, this required dutiful giving on the attendees' part, irrespective of affordability or convenience.

The religious amongst the Andrew and Duro Generation left Nigeria with their convictions and started churches overseas. Not knowing any better, they continued in the customs of the churches back home, which suited the all-Nigerian congregation that attended every week. Most of these churches in Diaspora focused on the survival and success needs of the people, and encouraged attendees to give their resources for a hundred-fold return.

The commitment of the Andrew and Duro Generation to financial "giving", heavily stressed by the new prosperity-emphasising clergy at the expense of traditional Christian values, has not produced abundance commensurate with their expectations. At the same time, the promoters of these teachings, the clergy who receive the contributions, are unashamedly flaunting their "abundance" with new cars and designer clothes. The disillusionment that this generation feel is underscored by the sad deviation of many churches from the ancient values of love, justice and righteousness. Many churchgoers who once believed no longer do so; some have left the prosperity-emphasising churches for the more traditional ones, while many now prefer to worship in the comfort of their homes.

The *Disenchantment* of the Andrew and Duro Generation with religion is not limited to the Christians among them. Many conservative Muslims are ashamed of the extremism of fundamentalists and try to disassociate themselves from those who practice radicalism. They are asking questions of their clerics about the whole essence of their Islamic devotion.

A GENERATION THREATENED BY DIVORCE

Another phenomenon amongst the Andrew and Duro Generation living abroad is the rise in the rate of separation and *Divorce*. Coming from a society that, relatively speaking, values highly the place of family in community, they had to face the culture shock of widespread divorce in the West. Many arranged marriages hit the rocks. Even legitimate love-motivated marriages have begun to crack under the pressure of living in the West, with the divorce culture providing an easy way out. An observable trend that strains the homes of the Andrew and Duro Generation is one person accusing the other of being the cause for bad luck. Subtly, the pursuit of success is taking its toll in the home and affecting the next generation.

A GENERATION INHIBITED BY DISCRIMINATION

A common experience of the Andrew and Duro Generation in the West is *Discrimination* – literal or perceived. They have had to survive in spite of it, unlike their parents who escaped when they had the chance. Even though Western societies have become more integrated in the last two decades, the Andrew and Duro Generation still experience instances of institutional racism, especially in the marketplace.

With Barack Obama becoming President of the United States and the enforcing of Equal Opportunity Policies in the United Kingdom, it is obvious that the worst is over. However, in the psyche of many people, whether black or white, proper integration is still an issue. In many arenas, Equal Opportunity statements are not equal enough in practice. This stems, probably, from the challenges people have with cross-cultural interaction.

DISSATISFIED GENERATION

If there is one word that sums up the condition of the Andrew and Duro Generation, especially those living abroad, it would have to be the word *Dissatisfaction*. Those who are honest enough to admit it will confess that they are not fully satisfied with their lives. Two decades of pursuing a dream of success has not yielded much fruit.

Interestingly, the nation that the Andrew and Duro Generation fled when they were younger has, since 1999, managed more than a decade of democracy, imperfect as it is, and experienced something of a revival. At some point under the Obasanjo presidency, Nigeria's national debt was reduced considerably and some infrastructure that enhanced business development were strengthened (notably the telecommunications and banking industries). These developing sectors produced more jobs and business opportunities, which many Nigerians at home capitalised upon. The internet and satellite media also provided a platform for Nigerians to interact with and display their trade to the world. Suddenly, Nigeria, when compared with the Rat Race of the West, seemed no longer a dreadful place to live. It was fast becoming an attractive land of opportunity, one to which the Nigerian in Diaspora could not simply return.

If there is one word that sums up the condition of the Andrew and Duro Generation, especially those living abroad, it would have to be the word *Dissatisfaction*.

Today, the feeling of entrapment and the lack of fulfilment continue to gnaw at the soul of the overseas-based Andrew and Duro Generation. These managed to run away from one challenge only to step into another. To date, their dreams of success are not yet *fully* realised.

OTHER D FACTORS

The Andrew and Duro Generation is now at the age when the body is more prone to *Disease* (and for this reason, Nigerians in Diaspora will think twice before leaving the Western World with its superior medical facilities). Dissatisfaction is leading to *Depression* – a condition that many suffer but do not readily admit.

All these *D Factors* lead me to label the Andrew and Duro Generation, my generation, especially but not limited to those living outside Nigeria, the D Generation (or Generation D). Of course, many are *Diligent*, *Determined* and *Disciplined*; our experiences and characteristics are not all negative. However, generally, we have to acknowledge that we are not where we dreamt we would be twenty-five years ago. The many expectations of a breakthrough are fast becoming a breakdown.

Probably the biggest issue facing Nigeria's Generation D is the age factor. Slowly but surely, we have clocked up the years and are now in mid-life. This is the age of reflection, a time for making serious decisions. Andrew and Duro are no longer children. They are about to have a mid-life crisis!

Section 2

REALITY

Chapter 4

IT IS HALFTIME!

Nigeria's Generation D "checked out" of the country from the mid 80s and throughout the 90s. They were in their late teens and early twenties at the time. Now they are celebrating their fortieth and fiftieth birthdays. Whilst these milestones are usually joyous ceremonies amongst Nigerians, the D Generation are not enthusiastic about the opportunity to party. Their attitude to "celebration" depends on their *D-rating* – the way they feel about their life achievements to date. Understandably, many Generation Ds will decline an elaborate party to mark these transitory years. Their thinking goes along this line: "What is there for me to celebrate? What have I done in the last forty years that is worth celebrating?" Refusal to celebrate *in any way or form* may well be a deviation from the traditional culture of partying and unnecessary spending. It may also be the result of *Deep Dissatisfaction*.

Certainly, we should be grateful for the gift of life and for the wisdom gained in four or five decades. Many other Generation Ds, friends and colleagues we grew up with, are not alive today. Therefore, irrespective of the quality of our lives, gratitude is essential, even at mid-life. Notwithstanding, these inner concerns that disapprove any form of festivity, are signs of mid-life reality checks – or what the American writer, Bob Buford, calls "Halftime".

THE HALFTIME CONCEPT

Mid-life is the time when people become increasingly age-and-life-conscious. They realise that youth has gone forever and old age is just round the corner. Brushing their hair one day, they suddenly notice a strand of grey sticking out conspicuously. They hurriedly pull it out only to find two more a week later. Eventually, they give up uprooting their grey hair because the more they do so, the more the unwanted hair multiplies.

Body hormones are changing. The reproductive system, especially in women, is gradually shutting down. Just "yesterday," they were the youth of the hour; now, youths from their own loins are starting secondary school and completing university degrees.

Life has steadily changed around them, but they could not pay much attention because of busyness on the field. Well, it is now halftime for most of us! The referee is blowing the halftime whistle!

> **Irrespective of the quality of our lives, gratitude is essential, even at mid-life.**

Football is arguably Nigeria's national sport, and every football lover knows the importance of halftime. After expending energy running around the pitch for forty-five minutes, halftime is a much welcome break, a time of refreshing and renewing of strength. More than this, it is a time to review how one has played the first half and strategise on how to improve on the first half score. If a team is losing at half time, the statistical evidence of the first half will inform them on the game plan they need for the second half. To ignore the first half performance, both of oneself and the opposition, is presumptuous. To repeat all the mistakes of the first half is foolishness. Halftime is the one opportunity for rest, reflection and rectification.

As it is in football, so is it in real life. There is a season in the middle of one's life when one ought to take some time out and review how the game of life has been played so far. Nigeria's Generation D is now in that season, faced with two major questions:

How have I lived my life so far?

How do I want to live the rest of my life?

These two questions are confronting many Nigerians today. We cannot just shrug them aside. In fact, Nigeria as a nation is also in halftime and needs to reflect on the past fifty years of independence and the next fifty (I will discuss more about this national milestone in chapter eight).

The Bible records threescore and ten as the number of years human beings have to live on the Earth. Going with this allotment, a thirty-five year old person has already spent half his time in the world.[1] Advancement in medicine safely pushes this middle point to forty or a bit higher. If sixty or sixty-five is the retirement age in the workplace and active employment started at twenty five, then forty is the midpoint of one's earning years. At fifty, only a decade of active employment is practicable – and that is if the jobs are available. Chances of employment and earning ability drop the more one ages because of competition from the younger, more energetic generation.

All these make halftime a valuable interlude in the course of life. Nigeria's Generation D must make the most of this recess time.

There is a season in the middle of one's life when one ought to take some time out and review how the game of life has been played so far.

Halftime is not a time to take lightly. It does not last forever and there may not be another in the game. It is a time for tough questions and serious considerations. In the rest of this chapter and the next, I want to ask a number of questions that will help each Generation D to reflect on the last forty years. Whilst these Generation D factors are common experiences, the following is an opportunity for personal reflection. The following questions will, therefore, address *you* personally.

WHAT IS YOUR D-RATING?

Firstly, what is your *D-Rating*—the way *you* feel about your life achievements to date? How do *you* feel about yourself? Can you identify with any of the *D-Factors* discussed in the previous chapter? Self-judgement is a crucial step towards transformation. Use the exercise below to determine your *D-Rating*.

HALFTIME SELF-ASSESSMENT

(Exercise One)

Shade only the stars beside each D statement that you can identify with even in part.

1. Dispersed in Diaspora? ☆

I am a Nigerian presently living outside Nigeria (in Diaspora) and have done so for more than five years. I identify with Andrew who "checked out" because of the deterioration of the nation.

2. Desperate? ☆

My goal is to be successful in life and want to attain it by any means. The end (success at all costs) justifies the means.

3. Deprived? ☆

I feel that I was hindered by my parents and the circumstances in which I grew from doing what I really love. I have not pursued my dream career.

4. Disappointed? ☆

I feel let down by Nigeria's politicians and by all the people who have governed the nation since independence, both military and civilian.

5. Detached? ☆

I feel that there is little I can do to change things in Nigeria, having lived away from the country for so long. If not for friends and family, I probably would not think about the country for a long time.

6. Debt? ☆

I am up to my neck in debt. What comes in each month is barely enough to cover all my outgoings.

7. Dependants? ☆

Not only do I have children to cater for, I also try to help my siblings and ageing parents financially.

8. Deceived/Duped? ☆

At least once, someone, even someone from my family, has used false stories or blatant trickery to collect money from me.

9. Disillusioned? ☆

After years of faithful allegiance to my religion, I now feel a sense of cynicism and disappointment because the leaders have not lived up to their words and the morality of religion has been compromised.

10. Divorce? ☆

My marriage has suffered over the years under the pressure of survival. Even if I have not followed through with it yet, I have considered the possibility of divorce since getting married.

11. Discrimination? ☆

I have had much prejudice to deal with in Western society. It may very well be the reason why I have not achieved my dreams of success.

12. Disease?

I have more health concerns than I had twenty years ago and feel I need to pay more attention to my body's wellbeing.

13. Depression?

I have, in recent times, had bouts of feeling hopeless. I have more mood swings now than I had twenty years ago.

14. Dissatisfaction?

When I consider my life so far, I feel very discontented. I do not have the quality of life I desire. Where I am right now is considerably far from where I would rather be (or planned to be two decades ago).

Now calculate your *D-Rating* and shade in the result using the following formulae:

D-Rating = <u>Number of applicable Ds</u>
                                2

(If your "Number of applicable Ds" is over 10, cap it at 10)

My *D-Rating* = ☆ ☆ ☆ ☆ ☆

The outcome of your *D-Rating* calculation, ranging from 1-Star or 5-Star, is only an indication of your current state of mind when you assess your present life circumstances. It highlights some of the things you need to consider at this stage in your life. The higher your D-Rating, the more dissatisfied you probably are with your achievements to date.

Self-judgement is a crucial step towards transformation.

ANOTHER D EXERCISE

Here's another exercise for you to complete. The question is, *"How satisfied are you with the different areas of your life?"* Consider the following seven aspects of life and give yourself a score using the provided scale. Be honest with yourself and write the first number that comes to mind.

HALFTIME SELF-ASSESSMENT

(Exercise Two)

Use the following scale to assess yourself:

1 = Very Dissatisfied   5 = Can't complain

2 = Dissatisfied   6 = Satisfied

3 = Below average   7 = Very Satisfied

4 = Just okay

---

1. Finances

Consider the current state of your finances – your savings, investments, assets, preparation for retirement and liabilities. Now grade your level of satisfaction on a scale of 1 to 7.

❑1 ❑2 ❑3 ❑4 ❑5 ❑6 ❑7
Very   Very
Dissatisfied   Satisfied

2. Marriage

Consider the current state of your marriage – your relationship with your spouse and children, the atmosphere in the home, the sense of oneness and fulfilment that you experience daily. Now grade your level of satisfaction on a scale of 1 to 7.

❑1 ❑2 ❑3 ❑4 ❑5 ❑6 ❑7
Very   Very
Dissatisfied   Satisfied

3. Health

Consider the current state of your health – your fitness level, eating habits, exercise regime, amount of rest you give yourself and the health issues you are battling with. Now grade your level of satisfaction on a scale of 1 to 7.

❑1 ❑2 ❑3 ❑4 ❑5 ❑6 ❑7
Very   Very
Dissatisfied   Satisfied

4. Emotions

Consider the current state of your emotions – your sense of self esteem and self worth, tendencies toward depression, level of happiness and independence. Now grade your level of satisfaction on a scale of 1 to 7.

☐1　☐2　☐3　☐4　☐5　☐6　☐7
Very　　　　　　　　　　　　　Very
Dissatisfied　　　　　　　　　Satisfied

5. Spiritual life

Consider the current state of your spiritual life – your relationship with the Creator, convictions about and preparedness for eternity, consistency in spiritual disciplines and quality of inner life. Now grade your level of satisfaction on a scale of 1 to 7.

☐1　☐2　☐3　☐4　☐5　☐6　☐7
Very　　　　　　　　　　　　　Very
Dissatisfied　　　　　　　　　Satisfied

6. Social life

Consider the current state of your social life – your relationship with people, number of friends, the social circles to which you belong and your ability to enjoy the comforts of life. Now grade your level of satisfaction on a scale of 1 to 7.

☐1　☐2　☐3　☐4　☐5　☐6　☐7
Very　　　　　　　　　　　　　Very
Dissatisfied　　　　　　　　　Satisfied

7. Legacy

Consider the legacy you are presently building – your accomplishments, contribution to the development of community, acts of charity, the number of people you have affected positively and the things you will be remembered for when you leave this world. Now grade your level of satisfaction on a scale of 1 to 7.

❑1 ❑2 ❑3 ❑4 ❑5 ❑6 ❑7
Very   Very
Dissatisfied   Satisfied

Now add all your scores together

My Total Score = _____

Now multiply your score by two

My Satisfaction Level in % = _____

Use the following classification to award yourself a grade:

14% – 39% = E (Well Below Average)

40% – 59% = D (Just Average)

60% – 79% = C (Just Above Average)

80% – 98% = A (Well Above Average)

> **Your First Half Report Summary:**
>
> Score = _____%
>
> Grade = _____(A,C,D or E)
>
> Comment = _____ (WAA, JAA, JA or WBA)

Again, this exercise is just a personal overview of your life so far. It underscores the importance of halftime. From my observation and personal application, it would not be too far off the mark to conclude that the majority of Nigeria's Generation Ds are "Just Average". We are in the middle somewhere, not excelling and not utterly woeful. We are just maintaining the status quo and are settling for mediocrity. Well, the whole purpose of Halftime, the purpose of writing this book, is to provoke Generation Ds everywhere to review their lives and adopt a more desirable game plan for the future.

TRAILING AT HALFTIME?

In football, the score at halftime is not the final outcome. With a revised approach to the game and a renewed determination to winning, fortunes can turn around. The score at *fulltime* is more important than the score at *halftime.* Honest appraisals, tactical adjustments and inspirational team talk all happen at halftime, and can change the course of a game. We just need to recollect how Nigeria's Super Eagles won the Gold Medal at the 1996 Atlanta Olympics. We were trailing Brazil heavily at halftime and still went on to win the game 4-3!

Does it seem like you are trailing in life? Well, the game is not yet over! It is only halftime. Every Generation D of Nigerian descent has a lot of thinking to do, and there is no better time to take time out than now. Bob Buford was right when he noted that "during the first half of your life... you probably did not have time to think about how you would spend the rest of your life."[2] Now you have the time. You must *make* the time!

The average Nigerian is not accustomed to the holiday culture of the West. Generation Ds rarely saw their parents take any break from work. It is not something we were used to. Growing up in the West, however, has made the idea of holidaying more acceptable, if not just for the children. These have been times of leisure, relaxation and fun. However, the timeout that is necessary at this stage of every Generation D's life is more than a pleasure holiday. We all need a retreat of a lifetime, valuable time to think through the direction of our lives. To continue with a losing game plan in the second half of life, after poor results in the first, is a display of foolishness.

Let us not ignore the need for thorough appraisal. Even though some of the factors that possibly contributed to an unimpressive halftime score were beyond the control of many Generation Ds (like the greed of Nigeria's politicians, a visionless national government, global recession, racial discrimination, etc.), it is the responsibility of each person to make individual adjustments. We cannot entrust our destiny to outside forces that do not necessarily have our interests at heart.

We can learn from the looming ordeal of America's ageing *Baby Boom Generation* who, for the most part, are waking up to the shock of an almost non-existent Pension Pot and the possibility of a destitute life after retirement. People like Robert Kiyosaki, author of *Rich Dad, Poor Dad*, have attempted to flag up the issue and encourage a *shift* in the game plan of those affected. The *Rich Dad Series* were written to raise the level of financial literacy in people's lives and help them take control of their financial destinies. In a similar fashion, Nigeria's Generation D needs to apprehend their lives and quit hoping that circumstances around them will make the changes for them.

HOW LONG IS HALFTIME?

The amount of time required for adopti*ng* a new game plan in halftime will differ from person to person. First, time is required for a honest *appraisal* of one's life. Exercises like the ones above are helpful.

Consider a short break, perhaps a weekend, to think through your 'score sheet'. How have you lived your life so far? Do you have a sense of satisfaction and fulfilment about your life? You can also try and get feedback from people you trust. Ask them for their *honest* assessment of your life.

Secondly, you need to *acknowledge* your first half scores and come to terms with your score sheet at halftime. The more sincere you are with yourself, the less time you will spend at this stage. Do not get stuck in regretting past mistakes or missed opportunities. You can only learn from your past and move on; you cannot change it. When you acknowledge your successes and failures, you are getting ready to make adjustments for a better future.

Next, you will need time to rediscover and *apprehend* your true purpose in life, the true reason why you exist in the world. This is where considerable time is required, depending on the amount of knowledge you already have about your purpose. You may want to consider another break to engage in brainstorming and soul-searching. Even after the break, you may have to carry a pen and pad around with you to capture the ideas that come to you over a period. More will be discussed about this in the next chapter.

Once convictions about purpose begin to form in your heart, you will need to begin the process of *aligning* yourself with it by *accepting* and embracing your calling in life with all its intricacies. You will then set *new goals* in line with your purpose to which you will commit the rest of your life. True success is costly. It always requires dogged determination and the readiness to make sacrifices. This is where the shift of a lifetime that already started in the heart begins to occur in real life.

> **You can only learn from your past and move on; you cannot change it.**

Finally, you will have to devise and *adapt* a different game plan to *accomplish* your new objectives. With a shift in your paradigm in place and a commitment to running the race to the end, you can begin to make *your* transition from halftime to the second half of your life. Until all the previous steps are followed, transition will be difficult.

In the light of the above transformation process, it is important to reiterate that the amount of time each Generation D will spend in halftime will vary. It can be anything from six months to two years, whatever time is sufficient for the rediscovery of self and purpose. There is no point in rushing the process or prolonging it unnecessarily. The game of life is different from the game of football; so, you are not ready for your second half until you are truly ready. Hopefully, the following chapters will help you in getting ready for the remainder of your life.

Chapter 5

SURVIVAL, SUCCESS OR SIGNIFICANCE?

In his book, *Halftime: Changing Your Game Plan from Success to Significance*, Bob Buford attempted to help a generation of "successful" Americans face their mid-life dilemma. The widespread phenomenon he observed among the middle-aged, working-class American, something he had also experienced, was the sense of *dissatisfaction* that many feel even after evidences of success. The provoking question he asked himself was: *"After success, what next?"* The book, *Halftime*, conveyed the lessons he learnt and the concepts he processed when he *shifted* the game plan of his life from *Success* to *Significance*.

THE AMERICAN DREAM

The first half for the typical American is normally devoted to the pursuit of the "American Dream" and dominated by first half concerns, including "getting an education, entering the work force, starting a family, buying a house, earning enough money to provide for needs as well as a few wants."[1] This success drive permeates American culture. The Founding Fathers and freedom fighters of America believed strongly that prosperity and self-expression are the right of every citizen and they sowed the seeds of this mindset in the fabric of society through the 1776 United States Declaration of Independence, a portion of which reads:

> We hold these truths to be self-evident, that all men are created equal, that they are endowed by their Creator with certain unalienable Rights, that among these are Life, Liberty and the pursuit of Happiness.

Surely, every society has its own definition of "success" and each social class has a minimum parameter for measuring achievement. Instinctively, everyone aims to surpass the minimum success level by as many notches as possible. Success (or *appearing* successful), therefore, becomes an elastic target with an almost indefinite upper limit set by each individual. Those who have money and comfort want more of the same. Such is the common tendency of mankind (not just Americans) in the first half of their lives.

The administrative set-up of American society, and indeed that of other Western societies, enhances and promotes the attainment of these success ideals. Comparatively, it is far easier to live comfortably in the West than in most developing countries (if it were not so, countless immigrants, including Nigeria's Andrew and Duro, would have stayed in their motherland!). There are more employment and business opportunities, and the playing field is more even. You can ascend the corporate ladder, start and grow your own business, practice your chosen profession, devote your time to Civil Service, get involved in Network Marketing or engage in dozens of other legitimate ventures that promise a fortune. If you work hard and smart enough, you will attain your goal of "success" and have a few gadgets to show for your efforts. Surely, the "pursuit of happiness" is an aim that most people in America, irrespective of race or religion, subconsciously aim for in the first half of their lives, only to wonder in the middle of their lives that there must be something more than a comfortable life.

A SHIFT FROM SURVIVAL

Bob Buford's *Halftime* was an effective resource for Americans who were already "successful" and needed to embark on a second-half journey towards *Significance*. For the majority of Nigeria's Generation

D, though, the journey is from further back. It is, essentially, a journey from *Survival* to *Significance*. The first section of this book sought to establish this premise – that most Generation Ds strive for Success but in reality are trapped in the Survival Game. Even those who seem to have "made it" in life, either at home or in Diaspora, still have a "Survival" mindset. The top five percent (or one percent!) that are somewhat living in comfort are not necessarily fulfilled within themselves. They also need to make the transition towards Significance. The time will always come in life when one has to concede that material acquisitions do not equal fulfilment. The middle of one's years (or halftime) is a perfect opportunity to shift towards a more rewarding perspective. Leaving it till the end of life can prove disastrous and too late. The conclusion of someone who only labours for "success" is likely to be, "Vanity of vanities; all is vanity."[2]

So, if "Success" (or the notion of "Success" to which many Generation Ds subscribe) is all about the abundance of things that man can possess, what then is "Significance"? In what ways do the latter differ from the former, and why should *Significance* be the focus of the second half of life? These are very crucial questions to consider at halftime.

DEFINING SIGNIFICANCE

Simply, *Significance* has to do with *meaning* and *importance*. Used in the context of life, it is a function of *who* a person is by original design (meaning) and how he lives in relation to others around him (importance). Everyone in this life is created with a unique purpose (meaning) and with a lifetime of opportunities to be a blessing to others in a given sphere (importance). A person whose life's *passion* is a reflection of his original makeup, and his *pursuits* express his distinctiveness and benefit others, is on the road to Significance. Such a person is never taken lightly or overlooked in his or her sphere of operation, even after death. Such a person is distinguished in the minds of people because of the contributions he makes to their lives.

Everyone desires honour and respect *from* others. A person of significance earns it because of his service *to* others. True significance cannot be bought with money or demanded through legislation or intimidation. It is only bestowed after sincere service to humanity. The main difference between the person who is significant and the person who is irrelevant is in the benefactors of his life – those at the receiving end of his life's service. The pursuit of success as an end can easily be restricted to the benefit of self, while the pursuit of significance is always for the common good.

Everyone desires honour and respect *from* others. A person of significance earns it because of his service *to* others.

Twenty years ago, Nelson Mandela was freed from prison – after twenty seven years of imprisonment. His lifetime fight against apartheid in South Africa earned him worldwide recognition. He became a person of *Significance*, not because of the things he acquired for himself, but for the freedom he secured for others. Even if he had died in confinement, he would still be a person of Significance, someone worth remembering for many generations. How many would know of him today if his goal in life was to own a cocoa plantation and become the richest man in his neighbourhood? Here is a pertinent question every Generation D should ruminate over: *How will I be remembered when I leave this world?* If you cannot identify one thing you are currently known for, the likelihood is that you have not yet found your path towards significance, let alone having begun the journey towards it.

THE SUCCESS-SIGNIFICANCE COMPARISON

Before we consider some questions and exercises that can potentially reveal the "significance" path to the sincere seeker, further comparison between Success and Significance will prove valuable. Many, through ignorance, will abandon the pursuit of Significance for the pursuit of Success. In their thinking, Wealth equals Significance (or worse still, wealth can *purchase* Significance). Many people in the Nigerian society subscribe to this paradigm. Even if money secures honour in the short term, it will not last for long. The seemingly "longer route" to Significance is the price one has to pay to build a formidable life that has immovable rocks as the foundation. The success of such a person will outlive him for many generations. Shortcuts to success will eventually fall short of the mark of lasting legacies.

Picture it this way. If Success and Significance are portrayed as circles, Success will have a considerably smaller circumference than Significance (see diagram 1). Whoever seeks the kind of success that benefits him alone, will affect a limited number of people and forfeit a life of significance. It is clear that Significance does not fit inside the parameters of that kind of Success.

Success   Significance

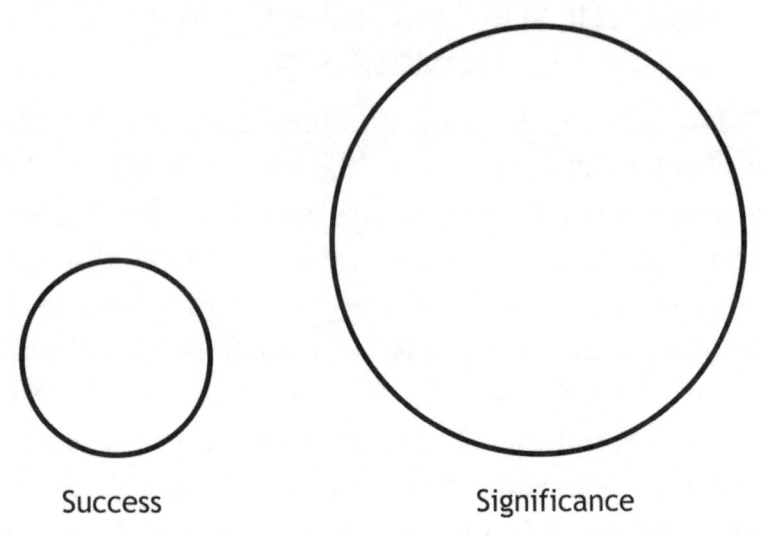

- Diagram 1

Conversely, whoever seeks the success of others will not only attain a life of Significance, but also become an automatic success because the parameters of Significance are large enough to accommodate the success of many.

Successes

Significance

- Diagram 2

Significant people help others get what they want and, in turn, get all that they want.[3] The order should be others first, then ourselves. This is why Nelson Mandela is celebrated the world over.

PURPOSE:
THE PATH TO SIGNIFICANCE

Of course, today's Generation Ds do not have to be freedom fighters to be significant. The fight against apartheid was Mandela's life call and that is what he will be remembered for. In the same vein, we all have a "call", something definite we were created to *be* and *do* in the world; a specific life work that requires the devotion of a lifetime; a vocation that generates a sense of belonging and significance in the world; a cause to which one can commit the whole of oneself; an *important* contribution to the general scheme of things. The pursuit of this "call" and the way it engages the essence of a person is what makes life worth living.

Which brings us back to the question: *What do want the world to remember you for?* Finding a singular answer to this question is an imperative task during your halftime recess. The world will not remember you for the wealth you acquired, but for the important things that you accomplished with your wealth. Your greatest asset is not measured in monetary terms or in length of days. It is *your* life. Your time.

The way you invest this asset in the second half of life matters a great deal.

Whilst trying to survive the first half of life, many people lose every sense of purpose they might have had in the past. Childhood dreams are abandoned. Lofty goals are cut to size. Natural talents remain unused. Time is spent on the mundane things of life. There is no decisive movement towards a significant end. This is true of many Generation Ds.

Your greatest asset is not measured in monetary terms or in length of days. It is *your* life. Your time. The way you invest this asset in the second half of life matters a great deal.

The demands of "survival", at times, do not afford us the time to reflect on the direction of our lives. Nine-to-five jobs are needed to pay the monthly bills. The requirements of growing children are a priority. Nonetheless, out of the rubble of first half busyness, we need to recover our life's purpose—the unique path to significance we are designed to take.

FINDING PURPOSE

The following halftime questions, I hope, will help you rediscover *your* purpose and calling and prepare you for a life of relevance to your generation. Give time and thought to each one and use them to sharpen your focus on your path to significance.

1. *What are you passionate about?*

Name just one. What is the one thing in life that you love and always wanted to do or get involved with? Most people are trapped in the Rat Race, working in jobs they do not enjoy only to pay their monthly bills. This is the Survival trap and it seldom leads to Significance. If you had the chance to do the thing that naturally arouses your passion, what would it be? Everyone is passionate about something. What is your passion?

2. *What are you indignant about?*

What are the issues that stir you fury? Sometimes, your anger is a clue to something you would like to change. Environmentalists, for instance, are incensed by the abuse of Earth's resources and devote their lives to its protection (the late Ken Saro-Wiwa[4] is an example that many Generation Ds will relate to). What are the problems you cannot stand?

3. *What are you good at doing?*

What is that one thing you can do so well without much strain? What ability or skill comes naturally to you? Is your current vocation engaging your strengths?

4. *What are you not good at doing?*

Are you forced by circumstances to carry out tasks that do not naturally suit you? What are the things you would rather *not* do because you are not good at them? Is your current vocation exposing your weaknesses?

5. *What are your past accomplishments?*

What are the tangible things you achieved in the past? What are the things you have accomplished that give you a sense of fulfilment? Apart from giving you a sense of worth, past achievements may reveal a trend and unveil areas of strength.

6. *What are your past mistakes?*

In what areas have you made mistakes? What are your past failures? This is not intended to discourage you, but to reveal any trend and unveil areas in your life that need strengthening.

7. *What problems have you consistently dealt with in the past?*

What issues have you had to face in life? In which areas have you constantly battled? Are you still facing these battles or have you found a way to solve them? The issues we consistently face in life are clues to our life calling. The solutions we discover to our problems are not just for us, but for others who are battling with the same kind of problem. When you devote your time to helping others solve their problems, life will become more meaningful.

8. What is the problem you are equipped to solve?

Considering your abilities, skills, gifts, experience and motivation, what is the problem that requires your expertise and involvement? Where can you make maximum impact in life? If significance is about adding value to others, then the problem you are best equipped and adequately motivated to solve is a strong indication of the Significance path you are to pursue.

9. What would you like to change in life?

If you had all the resources at your disposal, what would you like to eradicate in life? What benefit would you introduce to the world?

10. Who are you called to serve?

Again, if true significance is derived from serving others, who are you best suited to serve? What group of people require your expertise the most? Doctors serve their patients. Teachers serve their students. Councillors serve their constituencies. Presidents serve their nations. Who are the beneficiaries of your life's calling?

11. What do people know you for?

Can you name one thing you are consistently known for? When people in your sphere of influence think of you, what readily comes to their mind? Are you known for the value you add to life or the offence you cause to lives? What is your reputation in your community?

12. What are the unfulfilled prophecies of your life?

Which childhood dream are you yet to realise? What thing have you always wanted to do that you have not yet done? What are the promising features of your life that have not yet manifested? What goals do you have written down that are not yet attained? What prophetic pronouncement over your life is yet to be fulfilled?

13. What are you designed to accomplish in this life?

For what purpose do you think you are uniquely different from the other six billion people in the world? Why were you born where you were born? Why are you a citizen of your country? Why did you have the education you had? Why do you know the people you know? Are you conscious of the opportunities that surround you? Are you aware of your own significance?

14. What do you want your fulltime "scores" to be?

When you carried out the exercises in the previous chapter, what was your halftime *D-Rating*? What was your level of satisfaction about life? If you felt unfulfilled at halftime, how do you want to be at fulltime? What would you need to change now for you to be satisfied and fulfilled in old age?

15. What do you want to be remembered for?

What is the *one* legacy you want to leave behind after your demise? What kind of eulogies will people give during your funeral? What will you want written on your tombstone?

YOUR PLACE IN THE BIG PICTURE

The questions above and other related questions are serious issues to consider at Halftime. They will help you find your place in *The Big Picture* (see diagram 3). Ultimately, significance is all about The Big Picture, how you fit into it and the unique contributions you are designed to make in it. Like a unique piece in a giant puzzle, you have a void to fill in this life. Those who live to pursue success alone cannot see The Big Picture, neither are they conscious of their importance within it. There is always a larger context in which we must fit and no single person is big enough to be The Context. Each one must enquire from his Creator how and where he fits into The Big Picture. Halftime, when used appropriately, affords the opportunity to make this divine discovery.

Like a unique piece in a giant puzzle, you have a void to fill in this life.

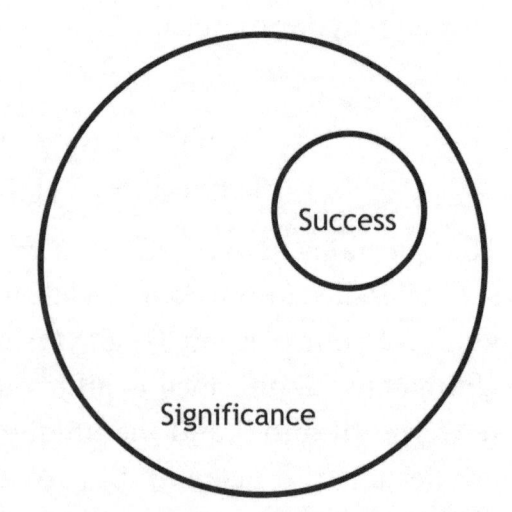

THE BIG PICTURE

- Diagram 3

As hinted in the previous chapter, there is no value in rushing through this halftime phase. You need to devote time to meditation, observation, consultation and prayer. Your goal is to arrive at a clear purpose for the remainder of your life, one that will establish your place in the Significance Roll Call and keep you motivated when the going gets tough. Until your purpose is clear, you are not ready to initiate the shift and rise to the platform of Significance. The next chapter will shed even more light on how you can embrace significance at this stage of your life.

Chapter 6

THE SIGNIFICANCE SHIFT

*E*veryone living in the world will at one point or the other, consciously or unconsciously, have to face the choice of setting either *Success* or *Significance* as a lifetime goal. This crucial junction requires a clear sense of destination. You cannot presume you will become a significant person in life if all you are living for is self. The path to Significance and the route to self-motivated Success are irreconcilably different. Nigeria's Generation D are standing at the Success-Significance crossroad. Each person has a decision to make. Are we going to continue with a Success-only game plan with the comforts of life as the ultimate prize or *shift* to the more enduring Significance game plan with the good of all as the aim? The truth is that, we all have one lifetime in which to make *The Shift*. What will you do at this junction? Your world is waiting for your decision.

The path to Significance and the route to self-motivated Success are irreconcilably different.

We have already implied that success that is measured in terms of personal wealth alone, the kind of achievements many pursue in the first half of their lives, is limited in its relevance to The Big Picture in which the global community functions. A person in pursuit of Significance, on the other hand, has a clearer view of The Big Picture and a distinct understanding of true success. He perceives, and rightly so, that true success is not the acquisition of material assets, but the sum total of things done for the betterment of others in The Big Picture. It is more than the desired destination of fame and prosperity, but the purposeful journey towards being a blessing to the world. The significant person may actually encounter fame and prosperity along the way, but these are not the *end* that motivated the journey. Even when there is no foreseeable prospect of fame and prosperity, the significant person is still fulfilled because of the benefit others derive from his life and the ultimate expectation of realising the intricacies of The Big Picture, having contributed significantly to it.

PASSION, MOTIVE AND THE BIG PICTURE

Consequently, some key factors that will determine the way each person shifts at halftime include one's *concept* of The Big Picture, *convictions* about personal purpose in relation to it and the *motivation* that links one to the other. The underlying desires (motive) residing in a person will form the rationale behind the inner vision he embraces (Big Picture concept) and influence both his game plan and the deployment of his abilities (convictions about the outworking of purpose). The way one sees The Big Picture (concept/vision) can also shape his inner longings (motive) and trigger a passionate pursuit of purpose (convictions). The person who truly discovers his purpose (convictions) sees it in relation to an all-embracing context (Big Picture concept) and is driven by a desire to realise it for the benefit of others in his sub-context (motive). All these three invisible factors—passion, motive and The Big Picture—are interrelated. They are key determinants of how a person will shift and the crucial decisions he will make in life (see the PMB diagram[1] below, diagram 4).

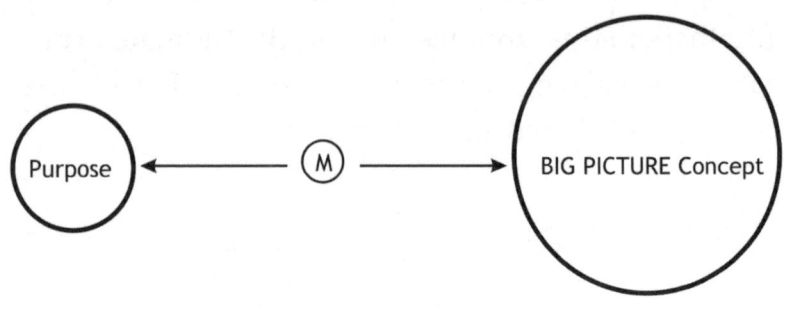

- Diagram 4

For instance, a person who is mainly driven by a desire to escape the hardships of life (his motivation) and attain a "successful" life of comfort (personal vision) will utilise all his resources – time, skills, opportunities, etc. – for the realisation of his ideal (achieving this goal become his life purpose). In the light of our understanding of Significance, this person is not only living for self, he has considerably reduced his perception of The Big Picture to size (or only sees himself occupying the whole of it). Everything else exists to serve *his* vision of comfort. His contribution to the society (The Big Picture) is minimal and done grudgingly (taxes, purchases, occasional voluntary services, etc.). His individual PMB diagram looks like the one below (diagram 5).

From Survival to Significance

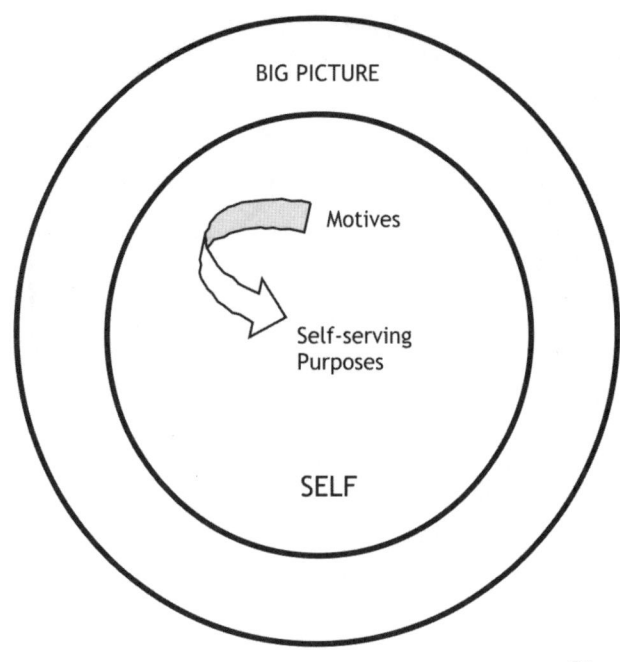

```
        BIG PICTURE

          Motives
          ↻
          Self-serving
          Purposes

          SELF
```

- Diagram 5

The life of a person motivated by greed and covetousness has a similar portrayal. He lives for self, even at the expense of others. Covetous people do not mind stealing from others in a quest to be "successful". At the end of their lives, when they reach fulltime, no one remembers them for good because they will not leave anything praiseworthy behind. If in answering the question, *"How would I want to be remembered?"* the above scenario is vehemently abhorred, then a drastic *shift* is recommended. A more desirable PMB diagram will look like the one depicted below (diagram 6):

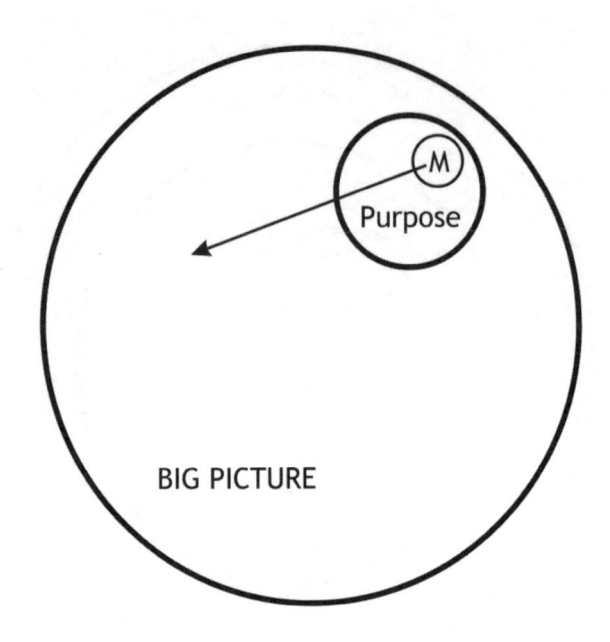

- Diagram 6

The person above is inwardly motivated by an aspiration to add value to The Big Picture, having found his place in it, and is committed to expressing his purpose to its maximum potential and serving the interest of others in his sphere of influence. His life benefits people other than just himself. When he reaches his fulltime, the world will miss him but his good works will become the subject of discussion and inspiration for many generations. Indeed, this is a noble goal that anyone can attain if they esteem the uniqueness of their purpose and are sincerely willing to live meaningfully. It requires a *shift* in the depth of a man's psyche, a shift in his paradigm. No significant shift will take place if it does not address the core values by which one lives.

SIGNIFICANCE, CORE VALUES AND OPPORTUNITIES

Success-driven pursuits that only seek personal acquisitions ignore the core values of justice, equality and fairness. The one who wants to succeed by all means does not really mind *how* he "gets to the top". However, in a Significance context, the *means* is as important as the *end*. Obtaining the sum of Twenty Million Naira is not admirable if the money was stolen or acquired through deceit. Significance-driven success will avoid questionable means and employ the core values of honesty and hard work, even if they seem "slower" than the shortcut of deception. In fact, the significant person will seek Twenty Million Naira in the first place because of the purpose it will serve in The Big Picture. The fundamental adjustment in a person's second half game plan, therefore, revolves around the subjects of purpose and core values.

Some questions were asked in the previous chapter that can give an indication of one's true purpose. Until a clear purpose registers upon the heart and mind, one is not ready for the second half of life. If the reason why you live is *not* to attend weekly parties or pay monthly bills, then what is it? Can you define it? You know yourself very well. Your Creator knows you even better. If, as previously suggested, you take time out to query yourself and enquire from your Maker how best you can serve your world, the understanding you gain will provoke a shift and align you with your true calling. It will also position you to choose wisely from the numerous options before you.

For instance, if a person is *only* thinking of how he can become successful in monetary terms, the options he will be considering at halftime are those that will achieve that end – a higher paying job, a career change towards a better paying profession, an internet business opportunity, a gambling syndicate that dreams of winning the national lottery, a fraudulent business deal etc. The person who chooses to be relevant in the world by embracing his discovered purpose for living sees opportunities differently. He will instinctively gravitate towards the ones that will help him leave his footprints of Significance on the sand of time; the ones that are consistent with his inner motivation to be a blessing to mankind (diagram 7).

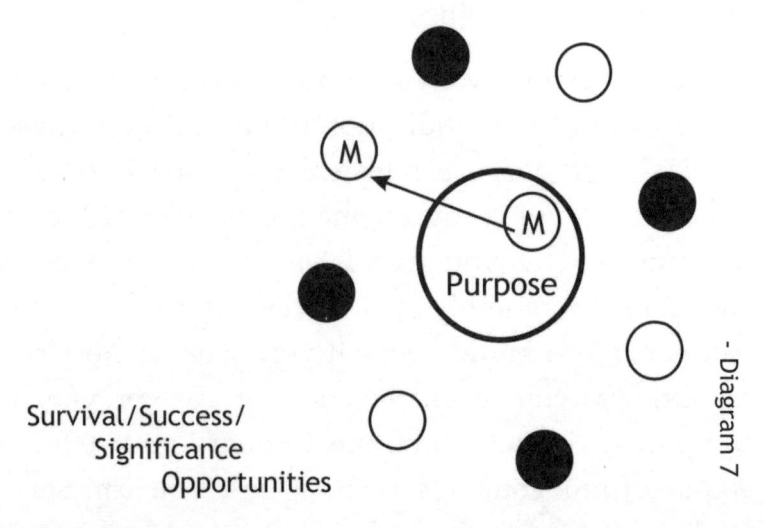

Survival/Success/Significance Opportunities

- Diagram 7

A person's purpose and the way he goes about maximising his opportunities are not isolated from his core values. If purpose defines *what* a person is wired to accomplish, then his core values are the guiding principles by *which* he realises it. These are the written and unwritten moral codes that undergird all his endeavours. In the final analysis, a person will always be true to the values that define his person. If true Significance puts the good of others before self, then the Significance-driven person will embrace the kind of values that prioritise the welfare of others. Ultimate significance and fulfilment in life require a person's values and actions to match, because when people hail significant achievements, they are also advertently referring to the quality of character that enabled the feats. Equally, selfish acquisitions, particularly those that take advantage of others, do not attract praise from people because of the undesirable values that inspire them. The shift of a lifetime requires a shift of values.

SIGNIFICANCE OF WELL-DIGGING

We can further comprehend the extent to which we need to change by considering the two kinds of people that exist in every society – those who dig wells and those who *only* drink from the wells. Their characteristics are as different as *Significance* is from *Survival*. The question for everyone to contemplate at halftime is: *Do I want to be a significant well-digger or a common water-drinker?*[2]

A person's purpose and the way he goes about maximising his opportunities are not isolated from his core values.

Let's go back in time. Around 2800 BC, in barren Palestinian lands, there existed two kinds of people – significant well-diggers and common water-drinkers. Everyone was a water-drinker (because no-one can exist for too long without water), but not everyone was a well-digger. The mere water-drinker was driven by the need to quench his thirst and that of his household, while the well-digger had a desire to satisfy the thirst of a community of people.

Requiring daily amounts of water to survive, the mere water-drinker spent his time looking for where he could go to fetch some. He depended on the nearby river for his daily need. When the water-level decreased because of draught, he sought the wells dug by others and joined himself to their community. The well-digger earned the right to rule over those who depended on his well for survival. He was regarded highly and given the respect he deserved. If he had a good heart, he made life comfortable for his people and sought to satisfy their needs. If he was a tyrant, he oppressed his people and enslaved their children in exchange for a sip of water. If he was a visionary, he trained his people on how to dig wells and create neighbourhoods, thus turning a barren land into a place of prosperity...

Which would you rather be: a soon-to-be-forgotten water-drinker or a good-hearted, visionary well-digger?

As it was in the beginning, so is it today. A significant well-digger has a different mentality from a mere water-drinker. He is a generational thinker who sees beyond the needs of the moment. He sees the benefit in delaying personal gratification for the pursuit of a higher purpose of serving others. He devotes time and resources into digging wells in the knowledge that his efforts will pay off in time. He shuns every opportunity to cut corners in the well-digging process because he does not want the wells to cave in under pressure. He is a systems-thinker who knows how to create procedures that others can operate long after he is gone. He earns the adulation of his community because of the value he adds to their lives. His work outlives him for many generations.

Which would you rather be: a soon-to-be-forgotten water-drinker or a good-hearted, visionary well-digger? Can you perceive the need to abandon the survival mindset of a mere water-drinker and adopt the significance paradigm of the successful well-digger? The former ends in destitution while the later leads to abundance for all. You choose.

Section 3

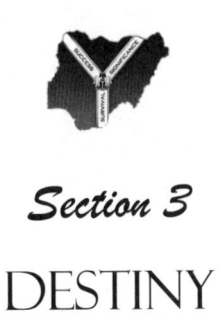

DESTINY

Chapter 7

LIFE BEGINS AFTER HALFTIME!

*H*ooray! A big congratulations to you! It is your fortieth birthday! And as the saying goes, *life* begins at forty!

After two decades of growing and academic learning, and another two of earning and child-raising, one is bound to be haunted with the need to have a rethink on life. This is a universal experience called mid-life, and the "rethinking" season is what we are calling halftime. Whether life will begin at forty for a person is dependent on how he approaches the question of his own legacy. Saint Augustine is credited with the notion that the question of your own legacy – *What do I wish to be remembered for?* – is the begin-

– *What do I wish to be remembered for?* – is the beginning of adulthood. This means that *life* does not truly begin until a clear answer to this provoking question is arrived at. Hopefully, the related questions put forward in previous chapters helped in the answering process.

In essence, you have not begun to live until you know precisely what you are living for. Taking it a step further, you have not begun to live until you know precisely what you are ready to *die* for. This is the beginning of life and a sure path to significance. Unconsciously, Nigeria's Generation D has sought for this path and now longs to begin real life. Even though Halftime is a shared phenomenon and Significance is a common destination, each person must find his own way, live his own life and make his own unique contributions to The Big Picture. The contribution we each make to life is the proof as to whether we lived or merely existed.

PURPOSE:
THE PLACE WHERE LIFE BEGINS

For many, *life* did not really begin in the first half. We merely existed by devoting time to the things that other humans deem important – putting food on the table, paying monthly bills, acquiring life's comforts, indulging in luxuries, etc. Expending our lives for the betterment of others, a key feature of purpose and significance, was not a priority. Making money was a more cogent concern. In the light of purpose, we were only *preparing* to live and had not begun to live.

> **You have not begun to live until you know precisely what you are living for... You have not begun to live until you know precisely what you are ready to *die* for.**

Your life begins with *your* purpose. Your life is not the survival scrap that austere circumstances confine you to or the success quest that popular culture drives you towards. Your life is the purpose for which *you* were created as *you* and not someone else. Once you find *your* purpose and commit wholeheartedly to it, real life can begin – and it does not matter whether you are thirty, forty, fifty or seventy. Of course, the longer you neglect the outworking of your purpose, the less time you have to leave a mark of significance on the planet. This is why a decisive move towards purpose is an all-important shift of a lifetime. You have just one life to live. There is no opportunity for you to right all your wrongs in another lifetime because no other lifetime exists than the one you now possess. What remains after this life is the assessment of humanity and Deity on how you lived, whether significantly or irrelevantly.

For life to truly begin, you need to crystallise all the halftime discoveries that you make about yourself into a *Purpose Statement* (also called a *Mission Statement*). Until you can pen down the reason for *your* existence in a few words, you are not fully ready for a cutting-edge second half. Your Purpose Statement will help you make necessary alterations to your current circumstances as well as filter the opportunities that exist around you. It is important to know from *where* and towards *what* you are shifting. Your Purpose Statement is a personal compass for this transition.

A decisive move towards purpose is an all-important shift of a lifetime.

If you have asked all the relevant questions (including those asked in this book), you probably have a degree of clarity about the *What*, *Why*, *How*, *Where*, *When*, *With Whom* and *For Whom* of your purpose. Your level of awareness and clarity will determine your readiness to formulate a Purpose

Statement. This declaration, beginning with the phrase "I exist...," should touch on several key elements of your findings. I cannot overstress the point that only those with a clear view of their purpose, evidenced by the crafting of a customised Purpose Statement, have a chance to live their second half *lives* to the full.

So, what is your life about? Why are you here? What is the ultimate goal of your life? To Whom have you been sent? How do you intend to serve them? Are you ready to craft your Purpose Statement? You may have to write and rewrite your Purpose Statement before it finally reflects what is in your heart. Until your heart jumps with excitement at the reading of your Purpose Statement, you probably have not found it yet. You can have a go below.

MY PURPOSE STATEMENT
I exist ....
....
....
....
....
....
....
....

Generally, in the first half of life, we lived other people's dreams and followed other people's agendas. We knew the vision statement of the companies we worked for and the churches we attended just because we were required to know and fit into them. This we did without considering our own *personal* purpose. At the time, fitting into other people's agendas really did not matter too much because within that context, our immediate survival needs were met. We earned a salary and met our social acquaintances. Now at halftime, the reason for our existence is top priority. Purpose must find its proper context of expression — not just any context. It now matters, based on your personal Purpose Statement, *how* and *where* you spend your life's energy and resources.

FINDING THE RIGHT CONTEXT

Take employment for instance. In the first half, we were more concerned about the monthly pay cheque offered by the company than we were with the pursuit of our purpose. In the second half, now with a significance mindset, it is important to consider not just the company's Mission Statement, but also how ours fit and contribute to it. In other words, for life to truly begin after halftime, we must define *our* context in the light of *our* purpose. If your present *context* conflicts with your convictions about *purpose*, then a major shift will be necessary sooner or later. Why continue working in a place that has nothing to do with your life's assignment?

Being in another person's context is not a problem in itself; the lack of fulfilment felt when the relevance of purpose is not realised within the context is the issue. Not everyone will start a company (or an NGO or any other corporate context), but everyone working within the company should not only believe in the company's mission, but also find and value their own unique contribution to the mission – a contribution that they equally believe in and are passionate about. Remember, we are all designed to make specific contributions in a context bigger than ourselves – The Big Picture. Your purpose and the context in which you contribute to The Big Picture should be in harmony.

In a bus garage, there are many vehicles going to different destinations. With a definite destination in mind, you will only enter a specific vehicle. Your choice of bus will not be determined by its model or the comfort of its seats. You will listen carefully to the destination that the conductor is calling out before entering. So it is with purpose. Any "vehicle" (context) we choose should be heading for the same "destination" (purpose) that we intend to arrive at. When either of these clash, life is put on hold, even at forty. Consequently, one of two things is necessary for ultimate fulfilment: a change of "vehicle" or a change of "destination". In the spirit of our discussion, if your preferred destination is "Significance" and the vehicle you currently occupy is heading for "mere Success", then a change of vehicle is recommended (after all, you will not want to compromise and settle for "mere Success" as your life's destination). All you would need to do is alert the driver, stop the vehicle and get off at the next bus stop. Of course, if you were driving your own vehicle and were heading in the wrong direction, all you need to do is make the complete U-turn yourself!

Satisfaction from our lives' endeavours will only be derived when purpose is positioned within a suitable context and the context is relevant to The Big Picture. Until these three are in agreement, we will spend the second half of our lives going round in circles with the same old survival game plan (see diagram 8).

This is a crucial point: If you are not already positioned within a corporate context that enhances your purpose and serves The Big Picture, the need to find or create one that does will be a priority in your halftime ruminations.

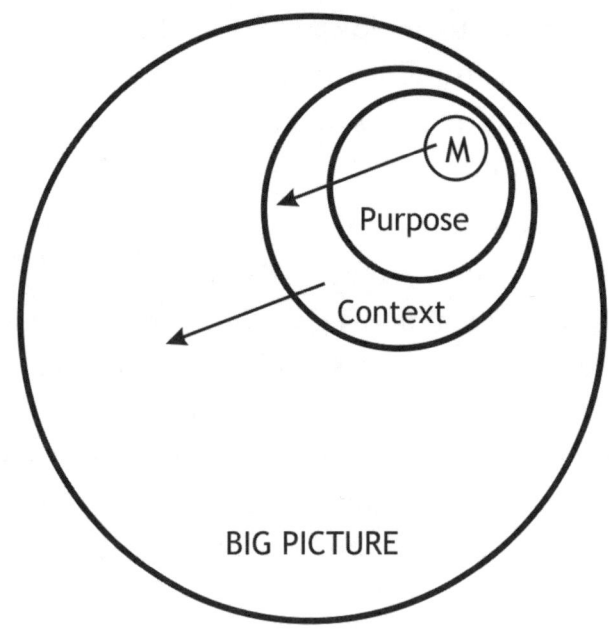

- Diagram 8

WHERE ARE YOU PLANTED?

Ask yourself the question: *Where are the opportunities for maximising my potential and attaining significance currently located?* This major halftime matter addresses the question of *where* to place your roots. Look within you. Look around you. Where are the relevant clusters of opportunities sprouting? What "Macedonian Call"[1] is presently ringing in the ears of your heart? Apple seeds do not grow in every soil. The conditions that make them bud are not present in every environment. If the life of that apple seed will ever begin, then the context in which it is planted must be right. Some plants start their life in a nursery and after an initial season of growth, are later transplanted to more suitable soil. Leaving them in the nursery or moving them to inadequate conditions will destroy any root system that exists.

In the same way, the seeds of significance that reside in you require the right environment. Continuing in a non-significance environment and hoping to end up a significant person is wishful thinking. If you want your second half to get off to a winning start, an environment that is conducive for the outworking of your Purpose is imperative (the more reason why the Purpose Statement you craft for your life must be clear and precise; it will serve as a lens through which you look at the environment around you and analyse the opportunities that come your way). Your life will be more fruitful and struggles will lessen, especially in the home with your spouse, when you are in *your place* of assignment. True prosperity begins when you find the place where you can function maximally.

Take a look at the diagram below (diagram 9):

From Survival to Significance

A Shift of environment
(mental, emotional, geographical, spiritual
values, principles, paradigm shift etc.)

LOCATION A
Survival/Success/
 Significance Opportunities
No Significance Opportunity
 that matches Purpose and
 inner Motivation
Environment to shift *from*

LOCATION A
Survival/Success/
 Significance Opportunities
Existence of Significance Opportunity
 that matches Purpose and
 inner Motivation
Environment to shift *towards*

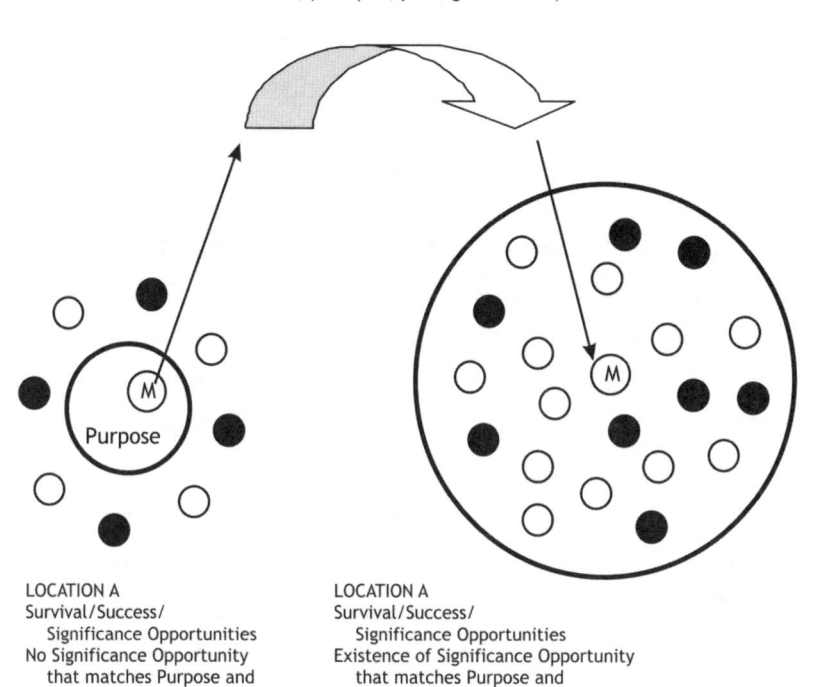

- Diagram 9

The person depicted in the diagram above is faced with a major decision. Where he is currently located, the mental, emotional, spiritual and geographical environment in which he functions does not draw out the best in him. Even if he has discovered his purpose, has an understanding of the section of society he is created to serve, and carries that awareness within, he is still not fulfilled because he is yet to find the proper context in which to pursue it. The opportunities around him are not resonating within him. He clearly needs to *shift*. First, he begins to shift within himself and embraces a paradigm that will promote significance. He is no longer comfortable with old friends with survival mindsets. He ceases to derive any satisfaction from his current employment. He feels there is something better for him "out there."

His awareness of purpose should prompt him to find the people he is called to serve, *wherever they are*, and the one opportunity that matches his true passion, *whatever it is*. The longer he stays in Location A, the more frustrated he becomes. As he searches and prays, Location B comes to his consciousness and with it a conviction of where he ought to be. It may be a new workplace, a new country, a business opportunity or a cause to get involved with. The more he thinks of Location B, the more excited he gets. It engages him, keeps him awake at night, dominates his conversations and permeates his thoughts. He finally overcomes the fear of the unknown and begins his new life after halftime.

Where are the opportunities for maximising your potential and attaining significance currently located?

INTERNAL AND EXTERNAL ENVIRONMENT

Your shift towards a new life will resemble the picture above and be unique to you. It is an environmental shift that starts from inside you. As discussed in the previous chapter, it starts from your values. What are the values that guide your life? Do you prioritise integrity, honesty, diligence and justice? Are you self-seeking or wanting the good of all? What are the driving philosophies of your life? What is your view of success and achievement? These dimensions of your environment are unseen but significant. They form the most important part of the condition for fruitfulness in life.

Apart from the issue of values reiterated above, there are some other questions you need thorough answers for as you begin life after halftime. Each one has a bearing on the shift that is necessary in your environment – whether internal or external.

First of all, *what are the things in your first half that you need to put closure to?* This is a very important point for every Generation D because you cannot keep on looking backwards if you want to make progress in life. You cannot re-live the past or live in regret of what was or could have been. It is time to move on. The first half of your life is over. The scores may not be good but you still have an opportunity to get things right. You are not too old to make a comeback in life. After all, it is only halftime. Therefore, forgive yourself for your past mistakes. Forgive others too. Where it is possible and necessary, take practical steps to make amends and repair broken relationships. Give yourself another chance and commence the journey towards significance.

With what do you feed your soul? What kind of things do you watch on TV and the internet? What kind of books do you read? It is fallacious to expect a significant ending in life with a malnourished soul. Your new life will require the right kind of inner sustenance. Leaders, they say, are readers, not just because they read but because of *what* they read. Refuse to let the myth that black people do not read be true in your life. Decide, instead, to edify your spiritual and mental self daily with books of eternal and significant worth.

What are your daily habits? Do you have established daily, weekly and monthly routines that foster a significant lifestyle? What time do you wake up in the morning? What do you do *after* you wake up? What is the last thing you do before going to bed? Many, I am sure, had poor halftime scores because of unhealthy and unhelpful habits. It is time to break every losing habit that you presently indulge in.

Forgive yourself for your past mistakes... Give yourself another chance and commence the journey towards significance.

It takes approximately thirty days to break a bad habit and replace it with a good one. Until you do something consistently for thirty days, you cannot call it a habit (which is why many New Year resolutions do not last beyond mid-January). Significant people intentionally develop winning habits and secure them through discipline and sacrifice. A new life at forty means new habits from now on.

Who do you spend time with? Who do you usually converse with? Who are the people that interact with your mind? If you constantly listen to survival lamentations, you will only fortify a survival mindset. If you associate with losers, how can you expect to win in life? Bad associations, it is said, corrupt good manners.[2] Choose your friends and colleagues wisely. Determine who will ride with you on the journey towards significance (presumably people travelling in the same direction).

What do you spend time doing? Do you spend all day on the internet (it is okay if it forms part of your work or adds value to your life and that of others)? Do you spend too much time talking on the phone? Do you spend more time daydreaming than you do actually working on your dream? You have the same number of hours in the day as everyone else. Make them count. Only those who have a clear sense of purpose *and* are devoted to accomplishing it will maximise the use of their time.

What do you spend your money on? What are the top priorities on your shopping list? Are you investing for the future? We have already highlighted the fact that the first half of life is full of purchases; all sorts of purchases, ranging from electronic gadgets, grown-up toys, social parties (with to-match outfits), life's luxuries and a host of other non-essentials. If you are particularly unhappy with your current financial statements, it is time to address your spending habits. A new life at forty means new spending priorities. Let purpose be the main determinant of how you disburse your cash. Significance will, from now on, require you to spend money on things that fulfil your purpose. It will also provoke you to divert some of your finances away from yourself and towards others who are the beneficiaries of your life's purpose.

Significant people intentionally develop winning habits and secure them through discipline and sacrifice.

Now, we come to an important question of purpose. *Who are you called to serve? Where* are they located? If you are a service provider, the people who use your service are the ones you are called to serve. If you manufacture a product, you are called to serve the people who use your product. If you are in Government, you should serve your constituents. In the light of finding and shifting towards the right environment for your purpose, you should attempt to narrow this focus even further — to a specific geographical location or a particular demographic grouping, for instance.

If you discovered at halftime that your fulfilment lies in your practice as a medical doctor, then your patients are the people you are called to serve. The additional enquiry you need to make is *where* in the world ought you to practice your medicine? You may be assuming it must be a top hospital in the West, when it might actually be a struggling hospital in a developing country. In the light of significance, it is not the monthly pay cheque that determines where we are planted, but the people we are destined to serve. The patients in the struggling hospital are likely to appreciate you more than those in the prestigious hospital. Besides, you may get involved in developing the health sector of a whole nation! As you think and pray about this question, the picture of your new life will become clearer.[3]

What new skills do you need to develop? Sadly, most people stop their learning after the last college examination paper. They fail to realise that learning only begins *after* college. Many professionals know this to be true. In a bid to survive the competitiveness of the modern workplace, they undergo tiring processes of professional development. However, beyond updating yourself for better prospects at work, you need to consider the areas of expertise that your purpose requires for you to be skilled. Do you need to go back to school? Do you need a second degree? Do you need specialist knowledge in your field? Any skill that you acquire in life today will always be an asset to you tomorrow.

Who are your teachers? Who is speaking into your life? Who is providing you with guidance? In order to secure a better result, football clubs sometimes change their managers and coaching staff. You may have to do the same. Over the last decade or so, the concept and industry of *Life Coaching* has grown considerably. The notion is now widely accepted that to reach one's set goals in life, some form of coaching is necessary. Nobody knows everything and everyone can do with a bit of expert advice. Mentors who are interested in *your* purpose and not just how you can serve *theirs* are invaluable. Experts who can instruct you on the next step to take towards your defined destination are helpful. Above all, make sure you are in tune with the Creator of all life and the Designer of your life. He knows your end before it began and is the best Person to guide you towards your significant end. This makes prayer an indispensible part of daily existence. Whatever else you do in the second half of your life, take time to pray for guidance.

Any skill that you acquire in life today will always be an asset to you tomorrow.

What are you willing to lay your life down for? For what cause are you ready to die? It is worth repeating that until you find the cause for which you are ready to die, you are not fully ready to live.

Significance fits this bill. Money and material acquisitions are not worth the cost of a life. They are subject to decay and depreciation. They are soon forgotten after one breathes his last. The only thing that will outlast a person is the one significant thing he lived for. The one thing he died for. The people he served with his life will remember him for generations to come.

Are you ready to shift from survival to significance? Are you ready for a brand new life? I assure you: no eye has seen, no ear has heard, no mind has conceived the doors of opportunity that will open for you on *your* path towards significance.

Chapter 8

CAN A NATION SHIFT?

Fifty, it is said, is now the new forty. It is also the upper age bracket of Nigeria's Generation D, which this book is examining. The same halftime issues facing those clocking forty are also facing those approaching fifty. The fifty year old Generation D, by virtue of his age and the time he has left to make a difference in life, may appear more desperate than his younger counterpart. No one wants to die in anonymity. Given the chance, the fifty year old Generation D will grasp an opportunity for significance with both hands. The good news is that, whilst there is breath, the chance still exists for those who will seek it out. Once found, decisive action must follow to prove the existence of desire.

NIGERIA AT 50!

As it is with individuals, so is it with whole nations. The political entity called The Federal Republic of Nigeria, fifty years ago, gained independence from colonial Britain, which officially classifies her as "middle aged". Even though this Jubilee year comes with a lot of festivity, it is also an ideal time to reflect on the past and prepare for the future. Knowing the Nigerian people, this unique opportunity to party will not be missed. However, we cannot afford to ignore the fact that we are in halftime and our halftime scores are not likely to be pleasing to the eye. In the same way that the individual Generation D, due to inner dissatisfaction about his first half performance, is generally not too keen on an elaborate party (even at fifty), the mood among Nigerians may not be upbeat when they consider the state of the nation. This is especially so when you examine the nation's *performance* in the light of her *potential*. There is a wide gap between what Nigeria has achieved and what she can achieve if her potential is fully maximised.

Figures and statistics do tell a story, but these are easy to manipulate and can easily mislead. That we are the second largest economy in Africa does not mean much to the average man on the street. Is there any reason to feel satisfied that our 2009 GDP places us at 44th in the world (out of nearly two hundred nations) when we have the potential to be in the top twenty?[1] If we grade our national performance by the experiences and perception of the general populace, how would we fare? It is people that make up the nation. Their perception is a more reliable indicator of our corporate wellbeing than the viewpoint of the minority ruling class.

There is a wide gap between what Nigeria has achieved and what she can achieve if her potential is fully maximised.

So, it is reflection time for Nigeria. How have we turned out after fifty years of self-government? It is not my intention in this chapter to create a catalogue of Nigeria's widely-acknowledged mediocre performances and under-achievements. We all know our plight so well. The multiplied thousands of Generation Ds around the world are victims of Nigeria's failures. So are their children, especially those residing in the Republic. After a mixture of military coups and democracy stints, the once promising and prosperous nation of the 70s has fallen to depths of economic decadence at the hands of overtly covetous leaders. Infrastructure is dilapidating; education standards are at best, stagnating; corruption is sky-rocketing; politics is decaying; the cost of living is soaring; and our foreign image is worsening. Much good has happened, of course, but the bad seems to outweigh the good (and bad reports travel faster and further than good reports). Unscrupulous acts of those in government undo the little done by those who precede them. For those who can afford it, private generators are the stable provider of power in the home, while the occasional transmission from the nation's *Power Holding Company*[2] is a transitory alternative. What more can I say?

Nigeria's Generation D has come full circle. They are raising another generation of single and dual citizen Nigerians who are beginning to reach the age of reason and rebellion. Has any of the issues that forced Andrew and Duro out of the country changed? What are the current prospects for their children? Would the coming generation have to "check out" for economic reasons as many of their parents did?

Instinctively, the Generation Ds living at home and abroad have many reasons to be concerned about the future of Nigeria after fifty years of independence. Unlike the period when they first escaped for their lives, there is a growing sense of responsibility to make sure the future is secure for their children on Nigerian soil. They cannot keep on running to other countries for survival. Besides, immigration policies in developed countries are becoming more stern. It is time to stand and make a difference in the land. What their parents could not do for them (partly, because of a fear of the military's bullets), they have to do for their children.

NIGERIA'S HALFTIME REPORT

Now, just as halftime for each person started with a personal report sheet to reflect the present state of affairs, a corporate report sheet for Nigeria is also necessary. *If* you were to write Nigeria's first half report sheet, how would you rate her? How would you grade her *actual performance* against her *potential to perform*? You can have a go below, using the following parameters and grades.

NATIONAL HALFTIME GRADE GUIDE

A = Excellent

B = Good

C = Just Average

D = Below Average

F = Poor

NIGERIA'S HALFTIME REPORT SHEET
(Circle the appropriate grade)

Subject	Actual Grade	Potential Grade
Politics	A B C D F	A B C D F
Economy	A B C D F	A B C D F
Infrastructure	A B C D F	A B C D F
Education	A B C D F	A B C D F
Sports	A B C D F	A B C D F
Electoral Commission	A B C D F	A B C D F
Medical Facilities	A B C D F	A B C D F
Military	A B C D F	A B C D F
Standard of Living	A B C D F	A B C D F
Per Capita Income	A B C D F	A B C D F
Homeland Security	A B C D F	A B C D F
Justice	A B C D F	A B C D F
Entertainment Industry	A B C D F	A B C D F
Religious Transparency	A B C D F	A B C D F
Media	A B C D F	A B C D F

Work Ethic	A B C D F	A B C D F
Patriotism	A B C D F	A B C D F
Excellence	A B C D F	A B C D F
Power Supply	A B C D F	A B C D F
Water Supply	A B C D F	A B C D F
Social Amenities	A B C D F	A B C D F
Maintenance	A B C D F	A B C D F
Transport	A B C D F	A B C D F
Civil Service	A B C D F	A B C D F
Freedom of Speech	A B C D F	A B C D F
Social Welfare	A B C D F	A B C D F
Wealth Distribution	A B C D F	A B C D F
Resources Management	A B C D F	A B C D F
Manufacturing	A B C D F	A B C D F
Telecommunications	A B C D F	A B C D F
Technological Development	A B C D F	A B C D F
Investment Opportunities	A B C D F	A B C D F

```
Business
Climate      A  B  C  D  F        A  B  C  D  F
Employment   A  B  C  D  F        A  B  C  D  F
NYSC         A  B  C  D  F        A  B  C  D  F
Tourism      A  B  C  D  F        A  B  C  D  F

              Summary of Grades
       Total As  ____
       Total Bs  ____
       Total Cs  ____
       Total Ds  ____
       Total Fs  ____

       Highest Occurring Grade  ____
```

I gave Nigeria a D Grade in Actual Performance, Just Below Average, and an A in Potential. I reckon that many of Nigeria's Generation D, out of sheer frustration, will give an overwhelming F grade for Nigeria's Actual Performance over the last fifty years! In either case, Nigeria's halftime score sheet is not too attractive. The gap between where we are as a nation and where we can potentially be is stupendous. The questions to ponder are: Can Nigeria shift and become a nation true to its potential? Can we move our level of national performance upward and close the gap on our potential? Do Nigerians have the desire and will to transform Nigeria into a nation of significance? These questions are pertinent and must not be glossed over.

The timeliness of these questions suggests that we are a nation in halftime. National events at the time of writing are strong indicators that our first half has ended and we need an urgent review of our national game plan.[3] If we continue the next fifty years with the same game plan as the last fifty, Nigeria will implode irreversibly. This is not doomsday prophecy. It is pure logic based on the evidence of our first half performance. To continue in the same old way and expect an entirely different result is madness.

THE NEED FOR CORPORATE PURPOSE

If it is true that we are in halftime, that our first half scores are grossly unappealing, and our inherent potential largely unrealised, then we need to maximise this time and establish through thorough soul-searching *where* we would rather be and *how* we can get there. What are our underlying problems and what needs to shift for them to be eradicated? We cannot ignore the mood of the masses, the facts of our own underachievement or the advice of our experts, and expect to perform brilliantly as a nation. It is time for candid, down-to-earth talk: we will either end up a nation that perpetually struggles to *survive* or a nation that is *significant* in world. Corporately, we are faced with the same issues that every individual Generation D is presently facing – the choice between Survival, Success and Significance.

Evidently, we have not yet, since independence, embraced a corporate vision for Significance. The Post-Independence Generation, many of whom are still pulling the strings of national affairs, have not yet proven they are driven by a significance objective. What they say with their mouth clearly contradicts what they exemplify before the masses. Selfish interests are put before national interests, and the culture of selfishness is being perpetuated throughout the land (as depicted in diagram 10).

We cannot ignore the mood of the masses, the facts of our own underachievement or the advice of our experts, and expect to perform brilliantly as a nation.

We have already established that success (or the self-centred kind of success) measured in terms of material acquisition, does not satisfy the seemingly successful. Only significance, measured in terms of duly-earned influence in society, is fulfilling in the long run and adds value to The Big Picture, which in this case is the nation. Those who attain "Success" through dubious means and at the expense of others go on to try and "buy" influence in society. When self-centred people gain societal influence through bribery, the sphere of their influence is full of corruption and, before long, a corrupt mindset is perpetuated by others. Such influence is short-lived and never ranks alongside true Significance.

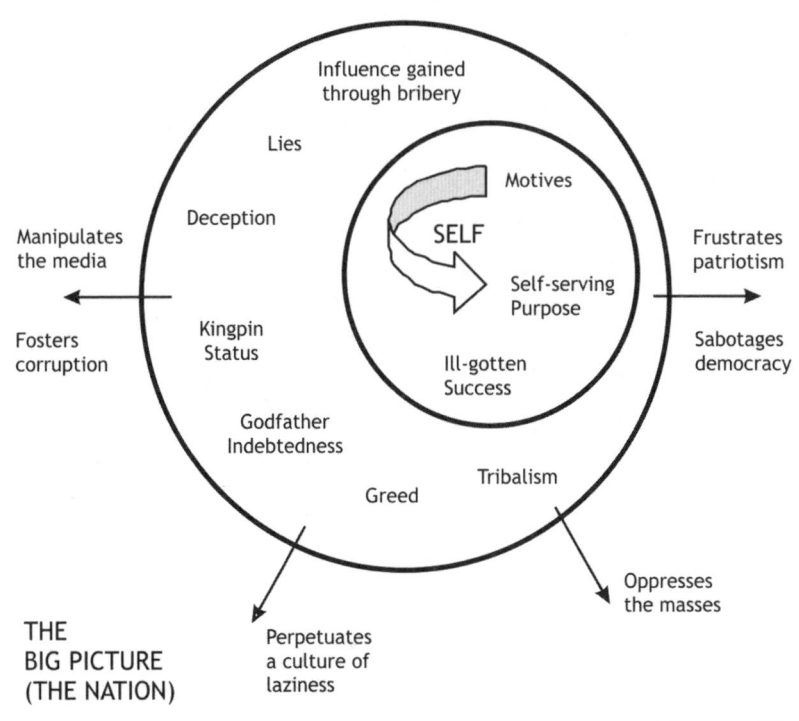

- Diagram 10

This is the unfortunate halftime picture of politics and leadership in Nigeria. The first fifty years of Nigeria's independence has been dominated by self-serving, self-enriching agendas. Instead of attending to the welfare of the whole nation (The Big Picture) and serving the interests of the public, the ruling class attend to themselves and gain influence among their own through monetary enticements. Their foreign accounts swell with the nation's wealth while the people suffer deprivation. The culture of corruption filters down to every level of society as more people desire a piece of the national cake. The Service and Manufacturing sectors suffer neglect and a drop in standards because of quick and ready revenue from oil trade. Infighting, favouritism and tribalism hamper unity and the democratic process. Nigeria thus becomes increasingly insignificant before its citizens and in the League of Nations.

The current state of affairs in Nigeria is the reason why we are positioned highly on the list of the world's most corrupt nations. It is the reason why some, in a bid to escape the rut of destitution to which the leaders have confined them, resort to crime, drug-pushing, fraudulence and other get-rich-quick schemes. It is the reason why Nigerian Generation Ds who have not inherited a culture of Significance and want to "make it" by all means can be found in prisons abroad. Why would there not be a professional brain drain on the nation when the

Nigerian work environment seems to reward the dubious and discourage the honest and hardworking?

At this halftime junction in our national journey, we need to define our preferred corporate destination. If we want to remain a nation struggling to stand on its feet, a nation that never attained its true potential, an impoverished nation forever striving to maximise its resources, then we need not do anything different from what we have done in the last five decades. However, if we want to become a significant nation full of respectable citizens, a prosperous nation that occupies a crucial leadership role in Africa and plays its part in the global context, then a major shift is compulsory. For every Generation D and the children they are raising, it is a shift of a lifetime, and there is no better time to change than now.

LEADERSHIP AT EVERY LEVEL

For a nation to shift, its leaders and people must be willing to shift. Moreover, the kind of shift that will qualify the nation for significance is not on-the-surface window-dressing. It must be in-depth and far-reaching. It will require a change of values and a shift in our view of success. The purpose and privilege of leadership at every level must become selfless service to others, which is the sure path to lasting significance.

Whilst it is easy to demand a shift from the nation's leaders, exemplary servant-leadership is required at *every* level of society. Everyone must shift and become a significant leader in his or her sphere of calling if we are to achieve national significance. Any reluctance on our part to change our current paradigm will render whatever else we do ineffective.[4]

> **Whilst it is easy to demand a shift from the nation's leaders, exemplary servant-leadership is required at *every* level of society.**

Say we divide the entire nation into seven spheres of activity (socio-spiritual sphere, politics and government, education, business and commerce, arts and culture, sports and entertainment, and media — see diagram 11), our path to national transformation will require stakeholders in every sphere to make the necessary alterations in the current *modus operandi*. Until every sector leader (and there are hundreds of sub-sectors in each sector) has the mentality of a significant well-digger and not just an ordinary water-drinker (see discussion on page 107), the sphere of leadership that they control will remain patched and lifeless. Those with a well-digger mentality understand the purpose of their leadership, which is to provide benefit for the community they serve. The "wells" that they succeed in digging, the corporate systems and administrative processes they put in place will benefit and serve the masses for generations to come.

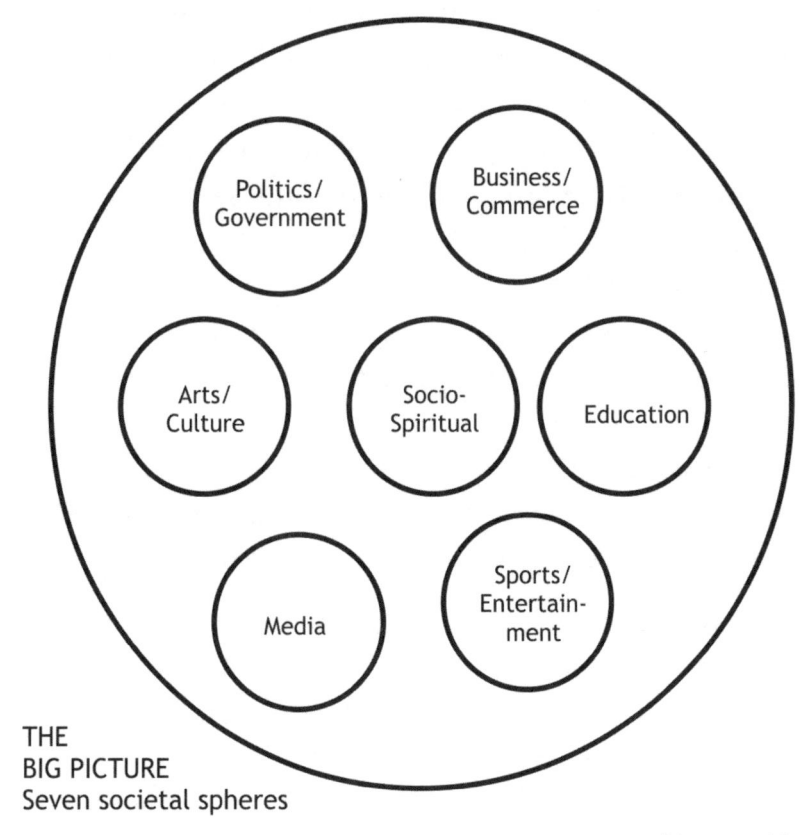

THE BIG PICTURE
Seven societal spheres

- Diagram 11

Take politics and national administration as an example. The Federal Republic of Nigeria is divided into thirty-six states and one Federal Capital Territory. Each state is divided into Constituencies that have representatives in the Senate (one hundred and nine) and the House of Representatives (three hundred and sixty), the Upper and Lower Houses of The National Assembly. They are further divided into Local Government Areas and State Ministries. There is the Federal Executive Council with Ministers who head various Federal Ministries, and Federal Parastatals that provide services throughout the nation. Summing all these together, a considerable number of people, multiplied thousands, are involved in running and delivering services to the nation. If all these people, starting from the President's office downward, embrace principles of significance, stewardship and diligent service, what manner of country will Nigeria be? If on the contrary, as it generally is today, the adopted ethos in Government from the President's office downward is self-interest at the expense of dedicated service, what manner of decay will permeate society?

What about religion? A global poll conducted by the British Broadcasting Corporation in 2004 showed that Nigeria is the most religious country in the world.[5] We boast of a nearly 50-50 Christian-Muslim divide, with a minority of others practicing traditional religions and a further minority with no religion at all. This means nearly 150 million people profess belief in God. Some of the largest denominations and churches in the world are based in Nigeria.

Each year, record numbers of people travel to Mecca on pilgrimage. Yet, is it not paradoxical that one of the most religious countries in the world is also one of the most corrupt? How can this be?

Simply, when religious leaders promote a Survival/Success message and neglect the message of Significance, the people pursue vanities and care less about their purpose in life or the values by which they live. This is evidenced by the almost non-existent social responsibility displayed by religious adherents and the bad examples portrayed by their leaders. Instead of teaching principles of service and helping people find their place in society, leaders are living flamboyantly, flaunting their material possessions and taxing the people in order to pay for their excesses. The people are constantly praying for the death of their enemies and looking forward to when they will have a success "breakthrough". What is the difference between this kind of religious leadership and the nation's visionless leadership? Until religious leaders become more significance-minded and take seriously the responsibility they have to exemplify a life and raise a people of significance, not only will they continue to be a part of the problem of Nigeria, they will forfeit every moral platform from which they can prescribe solutions.

When religious leaders promote a Survival/Success message and neglect the message of Significance, the people pursue vanities and care less about their purpose in life or the values by which they live.

The same scrutiny applies to all the other spheres of national activity and their hundreds of sub-divisions. In *every* pocket of national activity, we need *leadershift*—a shift in our leadership paradigm and philosophy. We need people with a significance mindset, who are living not just for what they can *gain* today, but for what they can *leave* tomorrow; people with national pride, who are devoted to the enduring values that make nations great. If this level of shift begins from the top down and meets the shift from the bottom up, Nigeria will no longer be the same. The fabric of society will undergo unbelievable transformation. The environment will become conducive for business development, foreign investments and the return of some of the Dispersed Generation. It all starts from a change of our national game plan from *Survival* to *Significance*. This shift will make Nigeria great (see the diagram below and compare with the diagram on page 143).

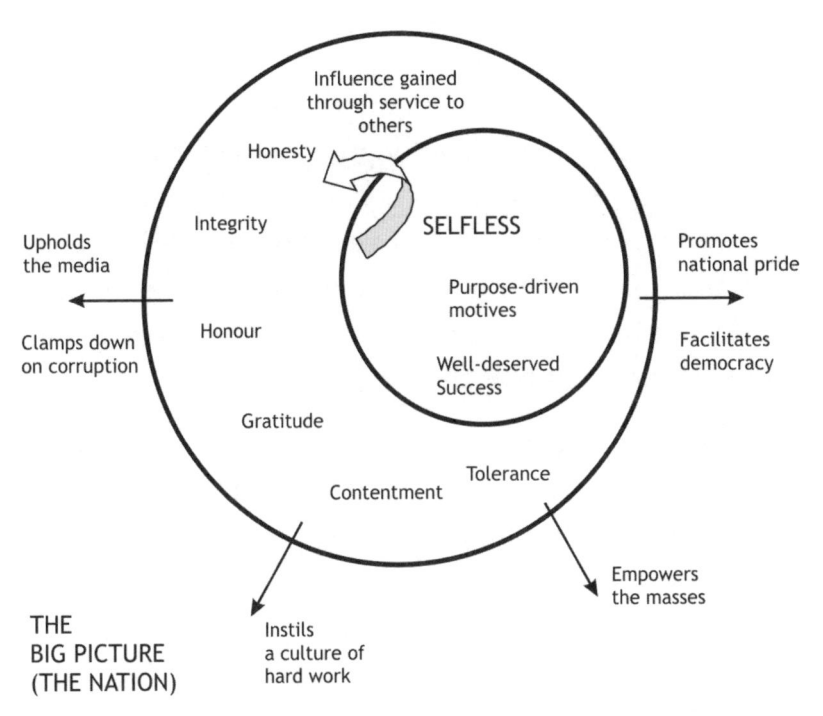

Diagram 12

Inner circle (SELFLESS): Influence gained through service to others; Purpose-driven motives; Well-deserved Success

Outer circle: Honesty, Integrity, Honour, Gratitude, Contentment, Tolerance

THE BIG PICTURE (THE NATION):
- Upholds the media
- Clamps down on corruption
- Instils a culture of hard work
- Empowers the masses
- Facilitates democracy
- Promotes national pride

NIGERIA'S TURN TO SHIFT

The answer to this chapter's question is, therefore, simple: Yes, a nation can shift from *Survival* to *Significance* if her leaders and citizens have a corporate vision to accomplish it, truly desire to change and are willing to pay the price. The price is clear: national interest must supersede personal ambition. This is the singular price everyone needs to pay. Is it too high a cost? If other nations around the world can shift, so can we.

Since gaining independence in 1965, Singapore has experienced a dramatic shift from being a third world country to her present state as the world's fifth wealthiest country.[6] The ongoing transformation in our neighbours, Ghana, who gained independence in 1957 and began her fourth republic in 1993 is also provoking.[7] In both instances, visionary and servant leadership, commitment and hard work were some of the factors that have led to significance.

It is now Nigeria's turn to shift. Our *history* and *prophecies* are beckoning on us to abandon all frivolity and aggressively pursue our significant destiny.

Chapter 9

THE COMING TRANSFORMATION

In this final chapter, I want to take a further step in answering the question of the last chapter, on whether Nigeria can shift to become a nation of Significance. My premise here is simple: not only do I believe Nigeria *can* shift, I am convinced we are destined by God in these last days to be significant in the Global Big Picture, and every Nigerian has a part to play in fulfilling this destiny. The aim of this chapter is to quell every doubt in people's minds and challenge every Nigerian, the Post-Independence Generation, the Generation D and the next generation, to have faith in the destiny of Nigeria – a faith that will prompt purposeful movement towards change.

Some may raise immediate objections to the mention of *God* in the Nigeria saga. Some say God has nothing to do with the problems of Nigeria and we should just leave Him out of it. I disagree. We cannot leave God out of Nigeria. Not only are we the nation that acknowledges God the most, we make mention of Him every time we sing our National Anthem and recite the National Pledge.[1] The last line of the National Pledge reads, "So help me God". Moreover, at Aso Rock, the seat of Central Government, there are notable national places of worship and prayer, one for Christians and a few for Muslims.[2] We are, therefore, a nation that professes belief. However, it is one thing to profess faith and another thing to *truly* believe. Do you believe in the destiny of Nigeria? Do you believe that we can turn around our national disgrace? Do you believe you can make a significant difference to the final outcome of Nigeria's unfolding story? I hope to make a believer out of you by the end of this chapter.

INSPIRED BELIEF

If we are not ready to believe in Nigeria's impending national shift and act decisively to make it happen, our retardation will become irreversible. We have to believe and thereafter act *because* we believe; not act unconvincingly and then hope for a miraculous intervention from the skies. The "miracle" we need will only come when our collective persuasion about our preferred destination spurs corporate action in the same direction.

> **We cannot leave God out of Nigeria. Not only are we the nation that acknowledges God the most, we make mention of Him every time we sing our National Anthem and recite the National Pledge.**

What is the point of turning up for the second half of a game if there is no conviction that the game can *still* be won? An irredeemable first half score, you may say. The truth is that, no situation is "irredeemable" if there is a *will* to turn it around.

Just over two decades ago, in February 1989, Nigeria's Under-20 national team were playing Russia's Under-20 for a place in the Semi Final of the FIFA *World Youth Championship* in Saudi Arabia. By half-time, Nigeria was two-nil down. To make matters worse, thirteen minutes into the second half, Russia had doubled their lead. A four-nil deficit with only thirty minutes remaining is enough reason to give up the hopes of progressing, but not our boys. Somehow, they were able to dig deep, inspire belief and revive their hopes of success. They registered their first goal on the sixty-first minute and went on to draw level by fulltime. They were still level after extra time and went on to score all five of their penalty shots. The "irredeemable" situation was gloriously redeemed and we got the Semi Final ticket, eventually coming second at the end of the competition. As previously mentioned, we repeated this feat in the 1996 Atlanta Olympics, coming from behind to win against Brazil and secure the gold medal. The point here is that we cannot afford to give up without a fight.

Doubt and unbelief have a way of draining enthusiasm and weakening resolve. They are evidence that we have no conviction about what we desire or want to achieve. They leave us too weak to dispel every contradiction of the mind. Until we deeply believe in our worth and destiny, we will continue to discard our chances of recovery.

CRITICISM VS. CYNICISM

Considering what Nigeria's Generation D have endured both at home and abroad, it is understandable that many are instinctively critical of Governmental policies and activities. And we should be. We have every reason to be critical. The right to freely express our views should always remain intact. The first thing that is curtailed by dictatorships is the human right to freedom of speech. As a nation, we have suffered many casualties of this category and abhor any return to those dark days of national repression and gloom.

However, it is one thing to be critical, and another thing to perpetuate discouragement through cynicism. When we give too much attention to pessimistic opinions, no matter how well-founded, an entire people gets inflicted with a spirit of defeat. Nigerians everywhere need deliverance from this demoralising spirit! You only need to listen for a few minutes where the subject of Nigeria is discussed. We are so quick to pinpoint her sore areas and highlight the legion of reasons why she is doomed to fail. We play the blame game and condemn the culprits. We may be right in our *analysis*, but are we right in our *attitude*? Many Generation Ds in Diaspora are scared of stepping on Nigerian soil again because of exaggerated stories of woe. We have lost all faith in the nation and have written off any chance of repair. We cannot begin our second half with heads hanging shabbily and shoulders shrugged indifferently. We have to believe, find something to hold onto, if we are going to win our national battle for Significance.

Many experiments have been conducted over the years to prove that unseen thoughts have an effect on seen realities. As a man thinks in his heart, so is he.[3] The wishes of a crowd, whether for or against, can affect the performance of footballers on the pitch. It is the reason why away games are relatively more difficult to win by visiting teams. Not only does the away team have to overcome their opponents, they also have to surmount the taunts of the overwhelming home crowd. It can get even worse if the outnumbered visiting crowd stop cheering for their own team. It is always counter-productive when supporters boo their own players on the field. Such acts only make matters worse.

When we give too much attention to pessimistic opinions, no matter how well-founded, an entire people gets inflicted with a spirit of defeat.

I am not advocating that we do not criticise our national players; I am only challenging an attitude that is too quick to criticise; one that *only* criticises and does little else. When all we do is to sound off critically at every opportunity, we are no better than the football spectator who, from the comfort of his settee, finds it the easiest thing in the world to tell professionals how to curl the ball into the net. Consistent condemnation can also turn us into naysayers who cannot acknowledge good deeds or discern positive change. Cynicism also damages our ability to express faith. We subconsciously become negative people who always see things negatively because that is the way we are wired. Even when we spend time praying for Nigeria, constant cynicism will cancel out any potential good.

> **Nigeria is destined for greatness and we must dare to believe this is the case. Our corporate conviction will inspire us beyond all the invisible barriers that have to date confined us to mediocrity.**

Unfortunately, circumstances have programmed Nigeria's Generation Ds negatively. Most of us have developed a survival mindset and will readily blame everyone else for it. It is time for us to reset our minds and shift our viewpoint. We need to develop fresh convictions about our common destiny. Nigeria is destined for greatness and we must dare to believe this is the case. Our corporate conviction will inspire us beyond all the invisible barriers that have to date confined us to mediocrity.

THREE AREAS OF CHANGE

There are three areas where I want to advocate a shift in our collective convictions. We need to believe *our prophecies*; we need to believe *our signs*; and we need to believe in *our personal and corporate responsibility* to make a lasting difference. After enduring a prolonged spell of national deprivation, we need to now receive the "sound" of the coming transformation with great expectation, believe the signs appearing in the horizon (no matter how small) and be ready to run with a sense of purpose towards our expected destination.

OUR PROPHECIES

Nigeria is a land of prophecy. Many prophetic utterances have been made about her destiny over the years. Discounting the general annual predictions that some denominational leaders make, most of which are questionable and uninspiring, I want to highlight the prophecies of a British missionary, Pa S. G. Elton, who came to Nigeria in 1937 and spent his entire life serving the Nigerian people from his Ilesha base. His life was an example of significance because he did not live for self but for the destiny of others.

He served and mentored many young Nigerians who later became notable in the growth of Christianity in the nation. What would make someone leave his own country of birth and invest the rest of his life in a foreign land, *our* country? He believed God sent him to live and die on our soil because of the glorious destiny he saw concerning Nigeria. Many prophecies about the future greatness of Nigeria and the role of Nigerians around the world are attributable to him.[4]

Pa S. G. Elton is the person who prophesied that Nigerians will one day be *significant* all over the world. This conviction was reinforced by the widespread prophetic notion about the positioning of Nigeria on the African map. I understood from my University days that "Africa is like a gun and Nigeria is the trigger." This meant that Africa has a role in the world and Nigeria will be the pace-setting, pioneering nation amongst the African nations. How inspiring this was for many of us Generation Ds back then! I reckon it should still challenge us today. Can you believe this prophecy? In many respects, it is partly fulfilled because Nigerians, the Generation D in particular, are in almost every nation in the world; they only need to discover the *reason* why they are there – for significance and not mere survival.

One other "prophecy" we need to consider comes from an unlikely source. Surely, God can speak through anyone He chooses. This prediction is not dated as far back as Pa S. G. Elton's. It was given in 2007 by the then newly appointed President of Nigeria, Umaru Yar'Adua, who was succeeding the outgoing President Olusegun Obasanjo. This prediction is today dubbed NV2020 (Nigeria's Vision for the year 2020). A derivative of this "prophecy" on the NV2020 website reads:

> "By 2020 Nigeria *will be* one of the 20 largest economies in the world able to consolidate its leadership role in Africa and establish itself as a *significant player* in the global economic and political arena."[5]

Notice the italicised words. "Will be" is a predictive tense. This is not a hope or a wish, but an objective that *will be* realised. "Significant player" refers to a position of importance and relevance. Is this not the message of this book, the destination that is beckoning to us all and requiring everyone of us to shift? Now, I ask again: Can you believe *this* "prophecy"? It would be foolish to discard the message because of any dislike for the messenger? If we do not embrace this corporate purpose, there is nothing definite for us to shift towards.

Seeing NV2020 as merely a Government programme doomed to failure would be a gross mistake. Imagine resuming a second half football match without any desire to win! There is something pathetic about criticising Government's activities while condemning its inactivity. NV2020, in my opinion, is an opportunity for us to establish a corporate purpose that will inspire us all in the same direction – towards Significance and away from obscurity. Call it by any name you want, now is the time for us to galvanise our collective will-power towards a more desirable end.

OUR SIGNS

For this purpose, I ask the second question: Can we see any sign in the sky? Is there anything happening in the nation that can inspire our faith? If, as advocated earlier, we shift our minds away from pointless cynicism, we will easily overcome the weariness of looking out for signs of hope. Of course, constant analysis of our many negatives can demoralise and drain every sense of belief. But let us look upwards a few more times and consider if there is any thing that gives us grounds for believing that our corporate expectations will not be cut short. Is there any development on the horizon that can fan the embers of hope within us?

I see many signs, little pockets of activity that are gathering as the fist of "a man's hand, rising out of the sea."[6] Before we know it, the clouds of change will thicken and unstoppable transformation will be our widespread and refreshing reality. The recent commotion around Nigeria's presidency is a point in question.[7] It is revealing the values and motives in people's heart, the desirable and undesirable. It is creating a demarcation between those who love the destiny of Nigeria and those who are bent on destroying it. Out of the prevailing bleakness, many encouraging signs are emerging.

"By 2020 Nigeria *will be* one of the 20 largest economies in the world..." This is not a hope or a wish, but an objective that *will be* realised.

Professor Dora Nkem Akunyili, Nigeria's Minister for Information and Communication,[8] is a sign in the sky. In the spirit of her previous eight years in office as the Director General of NAFDAC,[9] during which she courageously stood against illegal drug-trafficking in Nigeria, Professor Akunyili rode against the tide of fear and made a case for the morality of politics. After due consideration, she put her life and office on the line and wrote a pungent memo to the Federal Executive Council of Nigeria that was instrumental in steering the nation in the right direction. Her resolve was, "If I perish, I perish" – the kind of statement that only people of significance make.[10] I consider this a sign. Is she in the minority? Is she a lone voice? Not quite.

It was a sign of things to come when the *Save Nigeria Group* staged a peaceful march in Abuja demanding a respect for Nigeria's constitution – a feat that was replicated by hundreds of Nigerians in the UK and USA. Led by Nobel Prize winner, Professor Wole Soyinka, and outspoken cleric, Pastor Tunde Bakare, this mass protest, themed *Enough is Enough!*, was a sign of changing times in Nigeria. The voice of the masses will no longer be quietened at the face of political malpractices.[11]

I consider it a sign that a group of young Northerners, the *Northern Youths Coalition*, are condemning the self-interest of the older generation of Northern politicians. An extract from their statement reads:

> "There is a very clear determination on the part of old Northern oligarchs to preserve their power while delivering no benefits to the generality of our people."[12]

They believe electoral reforms will guarantee a smooth passage for politicians who can champion the cause of the public – a transition that self-interest politicians want to hinder by all means.

I consider it a sign of good things to come that Governor Babatunde Fashola of Lagos State is forging ahead amidst political opposition with his transformation agenda in Lagos and serving the interest of the public. He is providing others with an example of what State Governments can accomplish when they focus on delivering value to their constituencies.

It is notable that many Non-Governmental Organisations (NGOs) are springing up in Nigeria, championed by well-meaning Nigerians who want to use these corporate vehicles to serve their communities. Discounting the ones with dubious agendas of siphoning funds without delivering any public benefit, we cannot neglect this encouraging sign from the Nigerian grassroots.

The internet is a platform that is amplifying the voice of many Nigerians around the world. On a daily basis, encouraging signs of a growing clamour for significance and national effectiveness are evident.

When we consider all these and many other signs,[13] the sense of an unstoppable national shift becomes even more real. The skies are growing darker with clouds of refreshing change and an end of our national destitution draws near. For this reason, we should believe our prophecies and signs.

OUR RESPONSIBILITY

We now come to our individual and corporate resolve. This is where the rubber meets the road. The prophecies and signs are meant to strengthen our determination towards making a significant difference in the land. We must believe we can win this "game" and take our place of significance in the global community of nations. If we, Nigerian citizens, do not firmly establish a definite and positive corporate purpose in our minds, and receive encouragement from the signs pointing us in this corporate direction, we will become disheartened by the slightest sound of Jezebelic voices and discouraged by the divisive manoeuvres of self-seeking politicians; we will give up too easily on our individual races of purpose and forfeit our part in achieving our glorious corporate objective. In short, each Nigerian citizen in and outside Nigeria, the Post-Independence Generation and the Generations after them, should be determined to overcome every bureaucratic and political obstacle, and be a part of the future glory of Nigeria, our common Big Picture. In doing so, everyone wins.

As each Generation D at home and abroad rediscovers and refocuses on his or her individual purpose at halftime, it is not unlikely that some who reside in Diaspora will be prompted to relocate back to Nigeria in order to play a more active part. Many are already doing this. There is no sense in barely surviving in a foreign land if there are teeming opportunities to make a lasting difference in your nation. Nigerians in Diaspora have the benefit of two worlds. They have witnessed the state of affairs when things did not work and have enjoyed the relative comfort of societies that work. In addition, they have been a part of these working societies, providing services at civil and professional levels. They have seen the comparative transparency of Government in developed countries and the power of the law to which all politicians are subject. What is stopping Nigeria from working in a similar vein? Can it be possible that the present Generation D living abroad, some of them at least, has a significant role to play in helping Nigeria reach her potential for greatness? Two hands are required to lift a load to the head, it is said. The Nigerian at home and the Nigerian in Diaspora need to join hands together and lift Nigeria up. This is not a case of competition, but of complementation. There should be no conflict between the two Generation Ds because both are victims of the same historical mishap. The preoccupation of the moment should be how to transform the nation and what each person can do to achieve this goal.

There is a place where individual purpose and corporate destiny meets. Each person must find that place. For instance, out of the seven spheres of society (see page 146-147), to which are you called? In which sector does your sense of purpose, inherent gifts, inner motivation and interest meet? Where would you like to make a difference? Are you currently serving in this sphere of life? Are there opportunities in Nigeria to serve people in this sector? Are you sensing the "call" of significance drawing you homeward? Will you take responsibility for digging "wells" in your sphere and add lasting value to the community? It is worth repeating that the success of our drive towards a New Nigeria is dependent on significance-minded people who will provide visionary and servant-leadership at *every* level of society. Product and service providers should do the best they can possibly do for their customers and stop cutting corners. Teachers and educators should value the life of each pupil under their care. Government officials should serve the nation faithfully. Without any exception, everyone should contribute to the nation's progress.

Of course, not every Generation D will or should resettle back in Nigeria. This, however, does not exempt them from shifting towards significance or contributing to the wellbeing of Nigeria. When Nigerians abroad live unselfishly and provide servant leadership in their respective communities, not only do they add to the positive image of Nigeria around the world, they become a part of the fulfilment of prophecy – that Nigeria will be significant in the last days. The current negative image that many have about Nigeria will shift when we commit to serving our purpose wherever we are stationed in life. Out of our lives should flow the virtues of honesty, diligence and selflessness, for these are the virtues that make a people great.

CONCLUSION

Come October 2020, the age of the current Generation D will range between fifty and sixty. If you check your *D-Rating* in this pivotal year, how satisfied will you be with your life? Will your circumstances be as they are today or would they have improved considerably? Would you still be surviving or be known as a person of significance in and beyond your community?

The children of Andrew and Duro will be in their twenties and thirties by 2020. What kind of challenges will they be facing? Will they be thinking of "checking out" of Nigeria like their parents did? How would they view the prospects of their future? Would they be building their lives on a faulty *Survival* foundation inherited from previous generations or experiencing unprecedented progress on an inherited platform of *Significance*?

As a nation, Nigeria will be celebrating sixty years of independence by 2020. Would it be a well-deserved celebration at the back of improved standards of living and enhanced national infrastructure, or a landmark that only reminds us of our many failures? Would NV2020 be a reality or another failed political programme? Would Nigeria truly be significant in the global community according to our prophesied destiny? Would we have noble leaders who are selflessly serving the nation?

Of course, no one can tell what tomorrow holds. However, we can make adequate preparation for tomorrow and move towards it with confidence. It all depends on the objectives we set for ourselves today and the game plan we adopt to achieve them.

The Shift of A Lifetime has touched on a number of issues and left much to be discussed and acted upon. What are we going to do with the information and inspiration it contains? What kind of reality do we want in the year 2020 — and beyond? Would our children bless or curse us in 2020? Again, it all depends on the objectives that we set for ourselves today and the game plan we choose to run with. History will not forgive our complacency if we do not strive earnestly towards the mark of Significance that destiny is setting before us today.

May this message resonate in the heart of every truth-loving Nigerian. May every Generation D in and outside Nigeria embrace these truths and pass them onto their children. May our national leaders sacrifice their personal ambitions and relentlessly pursue our common purpose. Above all, may every person of Nigerian descent experience God's help as we press on to make this shift happen in our lifetime.

> I pledge to Nigeria my country
>
> To be faithful, loyal and honest
>
> To serve Nigeria with all my strength
>
> To defend her unity
>
> And uphold her honour and glory
>
> So help me God

History will not forgive our complacency if we do not strive earnestly towards the mark of Significance that destiny is setting before us today.

May the Lord, the Creator of the Heavens and the Earth bless the future of Nigeria and your future too!

APPENDIX

Below are the two National Anthems Nigeria has adopted since independence, and the National Pledge.

ARISE, O COMPATRIOTS (1978 – DATE)

Arise, O compatriots,
Nigeria's call obey
To serve our Fatherland
With love and strength and faith.
The labour of our heroes past
Shall never be in vain,
To serve with heart and might
One nation bound in freedom, peace and unity.

O God of creation,
Direct our noble cause;
Guide our Leaders right:
Help our Youth the truth to know,
In love and honesty to grow,
And living just and true,
Great lofty heights attain,
To build a nation where peace and justice shall reign.

NIGERIA WE HAIL THEE (1960 – 1978)

Nigeria we hail thee,
Our own dear native land,
Though tribe and tongue may differ,
In brotherhood we stand,
Nigerians all are proud to serve
Our sovereign Motherland.

Our flag shall be a symbol
That truth and justice reign,
In peace or battle honour'd,
And this we count as gain,
To hand on to our children
A banner without stain.

O God of all creation,
Grant this our one request,
Help us to build a nation
Where no man is oppressed,
And so with peace and plenty
Nigeria may be blessed.

NATIONAL PLEDGE

I pledge to Nigeria my country
To be faithful, loyal and honest
To serve Nigeria with all my strength
To defend her unity
And uphold her honour and glory
So help me God

JOIN US IN SPREADING THE MESSAGE OF SIGNIFICANCE!

We trust that you enjoyed reading
The Shift of A Lifetime.
Have you already begun to *shift* in your personal life? Are you confident Nigeria can experience a corporate shift and become a great nation?
Share your story and convictions by writing to:

shift@bookswithamission.org

You can also express your views on our Facebook page. Just become a Fan of *The Shift of A Lifetime.*

To purchase bulk copies for your group, please contact us at:

sales@bookswithamission.org

Tel: (+234) 703 6203291 in Nigeria

Tel: (+44) 7727 355000 in UK

ENDNOTES

Authors Preface

1. In December 2009, the President of the Federal Republic of Nigeria, Umaru Yar'Adua, took ill and was flown to Saudi Arabia for treatment. A prolonged time of absence, uncertainty about his condition and the delays in transferring power to the Vice President created a vacuum in government and led to growing unrest amongst the populace.

Introduction

1. Source: http://en.wikipedia.org/wiki/Generation

2. Nigeria's population, in excess of 154 million, makes her the most populous black country in the world, roughly the number of the second and third nations put together (Ethiopia, 79 million, and Egypt, 78 million). (Source: http://en.wikipedia/wiki/World_population.

Chapter 1: The Profile of Survival

1. This is an inclusive designation. Nigeria's "Angela" and "Dupe" are equally a part of what I, for convenience, have called "The Andrew and Duro Generation."

2. The Second World African Festival of Arts and Culture held in Lagos in 1977.

3. International Monetary Fund.

Chapter 2: In Pursuit of Success

1. The number 419 refers to the article of the Nigerian Criminal Code dealing with fraud.

2. For example, the Spanish Prisoner, the Black Money scam, the Russian/Ukrainian scam (source: http://en.wikipedia.org/wiki/419_scam).

3. National Electric Power Authority, which until 1st July 2005, was the regulator and provider of electricity in Nigeria.

Chapter 3: Generation D

1. General Ibrahim Babangida was military ruler of Nigeria between 1985 and 1993, while General Sani Abacha ruled from 1993 to 1998.

2. This is an overly conservative number. Uche Nworah, in a Study on Nigerian Diaspora, quoted Rena Singer of the American Christian Science Monitor (February 26, 2002 edition): "No one knows the exact numbers, but it is estimated that as many as 15 million Nigerians live outside the country, in neighbouring countries and across the African continent, in Britain and throughout the Commonwealth, in other European countries and in many Asian countries as well." (Source: www.globalpolitician.com/2682-nigeria).

Chapter 4: It is Halftime!

1. Fourscore years "by reason of strength" (Psalm 90:10). If this is a lower life-expectancy limit, "a hundred and twenty" years is the upper limit (Genesis 6:3). This makes forty and sixty the middle years respectively.

2. Buford, Robert. *Halftime: Changing Your Game Plan From Success to Significance* (page 19). Grand Rapids: Zondervan, 1994.

Chapter 5: Survival, Success or Significance?

1. Buford, Robert. *Halftime: Changing Your Game Plan From Success to Significance* (page 30). Grand Rapids: Zondervan, 1994.

2. Ecclesiastes 1:2 King James Version.

3. A maxim commonly attributed to American motivational speaker, Zig Ziglar.

4. Ken Saro Wiwa (1941 – 1995) was, amongst other things, a human rights and environmental activist who led a non-violent campaign against environmental damages in the Niger Delta region, especially for Ogoniland, his place of origin.

Chapter 6: The Significance Shift

1. *Purpose-Motive-Big Picture* diagram.

2. I introduced the "Well-digger" concept in my book, *The Secret of Abraham* (London: Sophos Books, 2006), and later in a novel, *The Greatest Well-digger in the World* (London: Sophos Books 2007).

Chapter 7: Life Begins at Halftime!

1. Acts 16:9,10 King James Version.

2. 1 Corinthians 15:33 King James Version.

3. I have intentionally refrained from writing about my

halftime experiences in this book. However, this point was crucial for me. Not only did I realise at halftime that I needed to reprioritise writing and publishing, I received a life-changing instruction from God to start my publishing work in Nigeria and be part of raising publishing standards in all of Africa. The moment I embraced this mandate, my shift became clear. I became more aware of the people I was called to serve in this phase of my life and discovered numerous opportunities for me to make a difference in my lifetime.

Chapter 8: Can a Nation Shift?

1. Source: http://en.wikipedia.org/wiki/List_of_countries_by_GDP_(nominal)

2. Power Holding Company of Nigeria succeeded NEPA in 2005.

3. Usually, the months leading to a nation's general elections are a kind of "halftime months" because during this time, the populace assess the performance of the current ruling Government and decide on which party's game plan they want to adopt for the next term. For Nigeria, the fourth democratic elections of the fourth democratic Republic (1999 – date) will be held in 2011. The months leading up to *this* particular election are "halftime months" during which Nigerians are assessing not only the performance of the ruling Government, but the nation's performance in the last fifty years of independence. They are also "halftime months" that are witnessing a call for reforms of different national sectors, especially reforms of the electoral process – electoral reforms that will ensure that the right game plan, the one voted for by the people, is adopted.

4. Since 2007, the Nigerian government has embarked on a commendable task of rebranding Nigeria. However, without a depth of change at every level of society as advocated in this book, these efforts will be short-lived. The same can be said of every other governmental programme.

5. Source: http://news.bbc.co.uk/1/hi/programmes/wtwtgod/3490490.stm.

6. This national shift is documented in the book, *From Third Word to First: The Singapore Story 1965 – 2000*, by Lew Kuan Yew, Singapore's visionary leader who spearheaded the change.

7. President Barack Obama's visit to Ghana in July 2009, his first trip to sub-Saharan Africa since taking office in January of the same year, underscored how far Ghana had come in national stability. The fact that Ghana enjoys uninterrupted power supply (compared to Nigeria) is just one of many indicators of progress in Ghana and an evidence of the corporate vision instilled by her past leaders, notably former president J. J. Rawlings. A sure wake-up call for Nigeria and Nigerians!

Chapter 9: The Coming Transformation

1. Both of our national anthems since independence, *Nigeria We Hail Thee* (1960 – 1978) and *Arise, O Compatriots* (1978 – date) have whole verses that petition God; the third verse of the former and the second verse of the latter (see Appendix for full lyrics).

2. The interesting story of how the place of worship for Christians in the State House, the Aso Villa Chapel, was established is documented in the book, *The National Altar*.

3. Proverbs 23:7 King James Version.

4. Ojo, Matthews. *The End-Time Army: Charismatic Movements in Modern Nigeria* (page 38), Trenton: Africa World Press, 2006.

5. Source: http://www.nv2020.org.

6. 1 Kings 18:44 New International Version.

7. Referring to the delay in installing Mr. Goodluck Jonathan as Acting President in the absence of President Umaru Yar'Adua due to illness.

8. For the 2007–2011 administration.

9. The National Agency for Food and Drug Administration and Control.

10. A statement first made by Queen Esther when she put her life on the line to save her people, the Jews (Esther 4:16 King James Version).

11. As at the time of writing, a number of protests have been organised by the *Save Nigeria Group*, including a large section of Nigerian Youths that were mobilised for an historic Youth Summit held on March 27, 2010. The theme was "Creating the Future." Source: http://www.savenigeriagroup.com.

12. Source: www.234next.com/csp/cms/sites/Next/Home/5532220-146/group_alleges_plot_against_ribadu_el_rufai.csp.

13. Since completing the writing of this book and before going to press, more signs have appeared. The Acting President Goodluck Jonathan's historic meeting with the US President, Barack Obama on April 11, 2010 is an example. The International Community are also looking out for our signs and I predict they will continue to multiply as we shift towards our collective destiny.

INDEX

419 *(see Fraud, Advance fee)*
Abacha, Sani *48*
Akunyili, Dora Nkem *164*
America *21, 81-83*
Augustine, Saint *113*
Azikiwe, Nnamde *30*
Babangida, Ibrahim *48*
Bakare, Tunde *165*
Belief *148, 154-156*
Big Picture, The *95*
Britain
    Colonial *29, 30, 42, 134*
    Right of Abode *38, 42*
Buford, Bob *64, 76, 81-83*
Calling *79, 91-93, 106*
Change, Three areas of *160*
China, Generation Y *22*
Coaching, Life *130*
Coalition, Northern Youths *165*
Corruption *44, 50, 143*
Crisis, Mid-life *60*
Criticism *156*
Cynicism *156, 157, 159*
Debt *52, 69*
Depression *60, 70, 73*
Destiny *24, 25, 77, 152-154, 162*
Diaspora, Nigerians in *41, 43, 48, 68, 167*
Disappointment *50, 69*
Discrimination *32, 57, 69, 77*
Disease *60, 70*
Dissatisfaction *58-60, 64, 70, 134*
D-Rating *63, 67-71, 95*
Elton, Pa S. G. *160-161*
Emotions *73, 123*
Equal opportunities *58*
Fashola, Babatunde *165*
Fawehinmi, Gani *35*
Federal Executive Council *148, 164*
FESTAC *34*
FIFA *155*
Finances *55, 72, 128*
Football *50, 65, 75, 130, 158, 162*
Fraud, Advance fee *44*
Fulltime *75, 95*
Generation
    Andrew and Duro *29, 34, 39-45, 47-50*
    D *47, 60, 63-66, 99*
    Next *(see Generation Y)*
    Post-independence *30-34, 48, 52, 142*
    Pre-independence *30, 31, 34*
    Studies *20-23*
    X *21*
    Y *21*
    Y, China *22*
    Z *21*
Ghana *152*

Giwa, Dele 35
God 19, 148, 153, 154, 160, 161
Halftime
    Assessment 68-75, 78
    Concept 164-167
    The book (see Buford, Bob)
Health 70, 72
House of Representatives 148
IMF 35
Independence
    US Declaration of 82
    Ghana 167
    Nigeria 29, 30, 50, 134
    Singapore 167
Kiyosaki, Robert 77
Kuti, Fela 35, 45
Leadership 144-152
Legacy 74, 95, 113
Mandela, Nelson 86, 89
Mission statement (see purpose statement)
Motive 101 (see also PMB Diagram)
NAFDAC 164
Naira 35, 39, 43
National
    Anthem 154, Appendix
    Assembly 148
    Pledge 154, 173, Appendix
NEPA 44
NGO 119, 166
Nigeria
    Civil war 23, 32
    Corporate vision (see Corporate purpose)
    Halftime assessment of 137-140
Nollywood 50
NV2020 162, 172
Obama, Barrack 58
Obasanjo, Olusegun 58, 161
Olympics, Atlanta 76, 156
Passion 85, 91, 101 (see also PMB Diagram)
PMB Diagram 102, 103
Power Holding Company 136
Prophecy 20, 160-163, 169
Purpose
    Context for 95, 96, 118-123
    Corporate 141, 142, 162, 167
    Statement 116-118
Religion 55, 56, 69, 148
Resolution, New Year 127
Rich Dad series 77
Save Nigeria Group 164
Shagari, Shehu 34
Shift, National 133, 154, 156
Shuffering and Shmiling 45
Significance
    And opportunity 105-107, 124
    And values 104-107, 125, 145
    Definition 85
    Shift 99
Singapore 152
Social life 73
Society, Seven spheres of 146, 168

Soyinka, Wole *35, 165*
Spiritual life *73*
Super Eagles *76*
Well-digger *107-110, 146*
Wiwa, Ken Saro *91*
World War II *21, 29, 30*
Yar'Adua, Umaru *161*

ABOUT THE AUTHOR

Israel Adetokunbo Emmanuel (formerly known as Adetokunbo Odulaja) began writing as a teenager after a dramatic conversion experience. He produced his first self-published book, *Sharing the Word of God*, at the age of nineteen and has since released thirteen other books and helped scores of other writers produce more than one hundred titles. Israel is the CEO of *Global Publishing Solutions*, the International Director of *Books With A Mission* and the Founder of *The Writers' Well*. Israel is also the convener of regular Writers' Seminars.

After his first degree in Computer Science with Economics, obtained from Obafemi Awolowo University in 1992, Israel relocated to London, United Kingdom, where he has been active in Church leadership and ministry development. As a Minister of the gospel, he is passionate about teaching the truths of God's Word and helping others find their purpose in life and society. In the spirit of *The Shift of A Lifetime*, Israel is now embarking on the task of establishing his publishing work in Nigeria and being a part of raising writing and publishing standards in Africa.

Israel is happily married to Linda and they are blessed with three children, Destiny, Daniel and David.

To contact the author or invite him to speak
at your church, civil or business event,
please write to:

israel@bookswithamission.org

- NOTES -

- NOTES -

SOPHOS BOOKS

*Raising the voice of wisdom
to all mankind!*